BIDDING AT BRIDGE
A QUIZBOOK

BARBARA SEAGRAM • DAVID BIRD

D0111741

Master Point Press
331 Douglas Ave.
Toronto, Ontario, Canada
M5M 1H2   (416)781-0351

Email: info@masterpointpress.com
Websites: www.masterpointpress.com
                  www.teachbridge.com
                  www.bridgeblogging.com
                  www.ebooksbridge.com

Library and Archives Canada Cataloguing in Publication

Seagram, Barbara, author
        Bidding at bridge : a quizbook / Barbara Seagram and
David Bird.

Issued in print and electronic formats.
ISBN 978-1-77140-018-3 (pbk.).--ISBN 978-1-55494-610-5
(pdf).--ISBN 978-1-55494-655-6 (epub).--ISBN 978-1-77140-804-2
(mobi)

        1. Contract bridge--Bidding--Miscellanea. I. Bird, David,
1946-, author II. Title.

GV1282.4.S4175 2014   795.41'52   C2014-906122-6
                                           C2014-906123-4

We acknowledge the financial support of the Government of Canada through the Canada Book Fund for our publishing activities.

Editor   Ray Lee
Copy editor/interior format   Sally Sparrow
Cover and interior design   Olena S. Sullivan/New Mediatrix

2 3 4 5 6   18 17 16 15
PRINTED IN CANADA

CONTENTS

FOREWORD

Is this book packed with all the best bidding conventions and instruction on how to apply them? Not at all! There are plenty of good books to assist you in that regard, including *25 Bridge Conventions You Should Know* and *25 More Bridge Conventions You Should Know*, both from Master Point Press. Instead, we explain the sound natural bidding methods that will allow you to play in the right suit (or notrump) at the correct level.

You probably know that there are many different bidding methods, or 'systems' — Standard, Two-over-One, Acol, Precision, and a host of others. This book is based on one of the most popular around the world: so-called Standard bidding. You have probably also learned that certain bids mean that your hand falls into a certain range of points. Remember, though, that bidding is an art not a science, and that counting points can be done in more than one way. So don't worry if we tell you that a certain bid means you have 6-9 points, when you have learned it as 6-10, for example; it's close enough. When we introduce technical bridge terms for the first time, they appear in bold type, like **this**. The Glossary at the end of the book has a list of these terms for easy reference.

Once your basic bidding is sound and accurately describes the hands that you hold, then you can begin to add special conventions that are designed to cope with specific circumstances. No one becomes a great bidder merely by adding conventions to their card. If you were building a house, you would start by constructing a solid foundation, not by buying a brightly-painted weather vane for the roof!

Each of the fourteen chapters begins with three or four pages of instruction. These are followed by several pages of multiple-choice bidding problems, illustrating everyday situations you will face countless times at the table. For each problem, choose the bid that seems to best describe your hand. You can then turn the page to see which bid we rate as best and an explanation of why.

When you have mastered all the topics described in this book, you can be confident that your standard of bidding will be well above average at your local club or in your social bridge games.

Barbara Seagram and David Bird

PART I

ONE-LEVEL OPENING BIDS
AND RESPONSES

1

THE OPENING BID

There are 40 **high card points** (HCP) in the deck. Since there are four players sharing these between them, an average hand will contain 10 HCP.

There are two basic types of opening bid. When you begin with one of a suit (1♣, 1◊, 1♡ or 1♠), 1NT, 2NT or the artificial strong bid of 2♣, you tell partner that you hold a better than average hand. You hope that your side can win the auction and reach a good contract. When instead you open with a weak two-bid (2◊, 2♡ or 2♠) or three of a suit, you tell partner that you have a good suit but less than an average hand. Your intention then is different. You want to take away bidding space from the opponents, who are likely to hold the majority of the points. Such openings are known as **preemptive bids**.

In this chapter we will look at the first type of opening bid. You hold above-average values, usually 12 HCP or more, and must think how best to describe your hand. A full description of your shape and strength may take two or three bids, sometimes even more.

long suit [not NT] ↓ ?

Opening with a balanced hand

When your hand is **balanced** (4-3-3-3, 4-4-3-2 or 5-3-3-2), an important rule of good bidding is to let partner know this as soon as possible. Around 80% of the world's players use the **strong notrump**, with an opening 1NT showing 15-17 HCP. This method, almost universal in North America, is the one we will follow in this book. If you happen to prefer a weak 1NT of 12-14 HCP, this does not affect the meaning of any bidding following a 1NT opening; it just means that the responder will need around 3 points more to bid a game or slam.

This is how you show a balanced hand, when your HCP fall into a particular range:

12-14	open one of a suit and rebid notrump at the lowest level
15-17	open 1NT
18-19	open one of a suit and jump rebid in notrump
20-21	open 2NT
22-23	open 2♣ and rebid 2NT
24-25	open 2♣ and rebid 3NT
26-27	open 3NT
28-30	open 2♣ and rebid 4NT

When two balanced hands face each other, a combined total of around 25 points will usually give you a good play for the game contract of 3NT.

Five-card majors

When you hold an unbalanced hand, or a balanced hand of 12-14 or 18-19 points, you will open one of a suit. A great majority of the world's players require five cards in their suit to open 1♠ or 1♡. This is the method we will use in this book. (If you happen to like opening on four-card majors, this will only affect a few of the quiz problems, so don't worry about it.)

Playing five-card majors affects your opening bid on a hand such as:

♠ K Q 8 2   ♡ A 6   ◇ A 10 5 4   ♣ 9 7 4

There's no problem on that one; you open 1◇, bidding your longer minor suit. An opening bid in a minor does not promise five cards and is frequently made on a four-card suit. Somewhat awkward are hands such as:

♠ A 9 6 2   ♡ K Q 10 5   ◇ J 8 4   ♣ K 2

You have to open 1◇, showing your longer minor despite the fact that it contains only three cards.

What if your minor suits are of equal length? With:

♠ A 4 3   ♡ A J 7 2   ◇ K J 3   ♣ J 6 5

you open 1♣ — the *lower of two three-card minors*. Suppose instead you pick up:

♠ K Q 8 2   ♡ 6   ◇ K Q 5 4   ♣ A 8 6 3

Now you would open 1◇ — the *higher of two four-card minors*.

Opening on a hand with two long suits

You thought this was meant to be a quiz book and you are itching to try the first problem? We understand, but let's first address the question of which suit you should bid first when you have two suits.

With a five-card suit and a four-card suit, *open the longer suit.*

♠ 9 5   ♡ 10 9   ◇ Q 8 5 4 2   ♣ A K Q J

Open 1◇. Do not think of opening 1♣. Note that the quality of your suit is immaterial — quantity is what matters. You plan to bid clubs at your next turn. When you bid two suits, the first one you bid always contains more cards, unless they are the same length.

With two five-card suits, *open the higher-ranking suit.*

♠ K Q 8 7 2   ♡ A 9 8 3 2   ◇ A 2   ♣ 7

Open 1♠. Plan to bid 2♡ next, allowing partner to choose between your suits.

Opening on a very strong hand

An opening bid at the one-level is not forcing. If your partner holds a weak hand, around 0-5 points with no particular fit for your suit, he will generally pass. When your own hand is so strong that you might make game opposite such a weak responding hand, you may open 2NT, showing a balanced hand of 20-21 HCP. Another option is the strongest opening bid in bridge: an artificial 2♣ (it says nothing about your club suit, merely indicating the power of your hand). This opening will always result in a game contract unless opener rebids 2NT, showing 22-23 points. The responder may then pass on a complete bust.

Measuring the strength of your hand

There are two important measures of the power of a bridge hand. The first is the number of HCP. This basic measure is fine on its own for assessing the strength of balanced hands. When you open 1NT, showing 15-17 HCP, your partner will immediately have a clear idea of what your hand looks like.

When you hold an unbalanced hand, the length of the suits is also important. Look at these two hands:

WEST	EAST	WEST	EAST
♠ A 5	♠ 10 7 2	1♡	2♡
—♡ A Q 8 7 4	♡ K J 3		
◊ 10 8 3	◊ J 9 6		
♣ Q J 4	♣ K 10 7 6		

West holds 13 HCP and opens 1♡. East responds 2♡. West has a minimum opening and passes. If a spade is led, the defenders will score one spade, three diamonds and one club. Declarer will make eight tricks for his contract.

WEST	EAST	WEST	EAST
♠ A 5	♠ 10 7 2	1♡	2♡
♡ A Q 8 7 4 2	♡ K J 3		
◊ 10 8	◊ J 9 6		
♣ Q J 4	♣ K 10 7 6		

Here West holds the same 13 HCP but he has slightly better shape. He holds six hearts rather than five. Consequently he has one diamond fewer. If a spade is led now, declarer will make nine tricks. He makes one more trick because he has *better shape*. Since he holds only two diamonds instead of three, he will lose only two diamond tricks.

WEST	EAST	WEST	EAST
♠ A 5	♠ 10 7 2	1♡	2♡
♡ A Q 8 7 4 2	♡ K J 3	3♣	4♡
◊ 10	◊ J 9 6		
♣ Q J 8 4	♣ K 10 7 6		

West still holds the same 13 HCP but he has even better shape than on the previous hand: four clubs and one diamond instead of three clubs and two diamonds. He now thinks that he can make a **game try** of 3♣. East accepts, bidding 4♡, and the game will probably be made.

The value of these three West hands was made up of two different factors: HCP and shape. Some teachers say you should add points for extra length in a suit, others add points for singletons and voids. Both methods work, so don't worry about which one you use (but remember that distributional values are only counted if you are playing in a suit contract, not in notrump). Simply stated, the more shapely your hand is, the more useful it is likely to be in the play, particularly if you find a satisfactory trump fit.

Opening Bid — Problems A

1.
♠A2 ♡J9862 ◇AQJ73 ♣10

What is your choice from these options?

(a) Pass   (b) 1◇   (c) 1♡

2.
♠985 ♡K1076 ◇A3 ♣AK74

Which opening bid is best from these possibilities?

(a) 1♣   (b) 1♡   (c) 1NT

3.
♠AQJ8 ♡1083 ◇KQ7 ♣A95

What bid is right here?

(a) 1♣   (b) 1♠   (c) 1NT

4.
♠10973 ♡AJ4 ◇75 ♣AQ94

Which of these three choices appeals?

(a) Pass   (b) 1♣   (c) 1♠

5.
♠432 ♡32 ◇QJ92 ♣AKQ3

Which of these two bids would you choose?

(a) 1♣   (b) 1◇

(The answers are overleaf.)

Opening Bid — Solutions A

1. 12 pts
  4   1   7
  ♠A 2 ♡J 9 8 6 2 ◇A Q J 7 3 ♣10

With 12 HCP and two five-card suits, there is no temptation whatsoever to pass. Should you open 1♡ or 1◇? The diamonds are much stronger but remember the rule that you should open the *higher-ranking of two five-card suits*. When you choose a trump suit, it is often important to choose the suit where you have the greatest combined length. Suppose you have eight or nine hearts between you. That will make a fine trump suit even if you are missing, say, the ♡A and ♡K. Also, it is important to seek a fit in a major suit rather than a minor suit. That's because you will need only ten tricks to make game in a major. **Answer:** (c) 1♡.

2. 14 pts
  3   4   7
  ♠9 8 5 ♡K 10 7 6 ◇A 3 ♣A K 7 4

Your hand is balanced and you therefore want to show this by bidding notrump as soon as possible. Should you open 1NT? No, because you don't hold 15-17 HCP. You should therefore plan to open one of a suit and to bid notrump at your next turn. You cannot open 1♡ because that would promise at least a five-card suit. Here you are happy to open in clubs. **Answer:** (a) 1♣.

3. 16 pts
  7   —   5   4
  ♠A Q J 8 ♡10 8 3 ◇K Q 7 ♣A 9 5

Your hand is balanced and you hold 15-17 HCP. End of discussion! You will open 1NT, giving an excellent description of your hand. When your hand is balanced, aim to bid notrump as soon as possible. **Answer:** (c) 1NT.

4. 11 pts
  —   5   —   6
  ♠10 9 7 3 ♡A J 4 ◇7 5 ♣A Q 9 4

Once again you hold a balanced hand. It is nowhere near strong enough to open 1NT. Should you open 1♣? No, because you have only 11 HCP and you are not worth opening the bidding at all. Some 11-point hands are worth an opening bid but only when they are shapely and contain a good suit or two. **Answer:** (a) Pass

5. 12 pts
  —   —   3   9
  ♠4 3 2 ♡3 2 ◇Q J 9 2 ♣A K Q 3

Open 1◇. If partner responds 1♡, you can now rebid 2♣. If you were to choose your 'better minor' instead (a common myth in the world of social players) and open 1♣, then you would be stuck for a rebid over 1♡. Bidding 2♣ at this point would promise more than four of them, and you cannot bid 1NT without a spade stopper. Bidding 2◇ would promise a very different hand (see p. 34). **Answer:** (b) 1◇.

Opening Bid — Problems B

6.
         7   4   3   14 pts — 1

♠2 ♡AK93 ◇QJ763 ♣K84

You pick up this hand. What action will you choose?

    (a) Pass   (b) 1◇   (c) 1♡

7.
        6   3   7   2   18 pts =

♠AQ5 ♡K7 ◇AK106 ♣Q982

Which bid is right from these four possibilities?

    (a) 1♣   (b) 1◇   (c) 1NT   (d) 2NT

8.
        5   3   —   5   13 pts —

♠AJ86 ♡K1083 ◇72 ♣AJ4

What will you choose now?

    (a) 1♣   (b) 1♡   (c) 1♠   (d) 1NT

9.
        9   —   3   12

♠42 ♡AKJ93 ◇9 ♣K10742

Which of these three choices do you like best?

    (a) Pass   (b) 1♣   (c) 1♡

10.
        3 1   4   3   11

♠K ♡J8754 ◇A10532 ♣QJ

What action will you take here?

    (a) Pass   (b) 1◇   (c) 1♡

(The answers are overleaf.)

Opening Bid — Solutions B

6.   ♠ 2   ♡ A K 9 3   ◇ Q J 7 6 3   ♣ K 8 4

You will nearly always open when you hold only 12 HCP, so of course you are happy to open here with 13 HCP. Will you open 1♡ or 1◇? There are two good reasons not to open 1♡. Firstly, such an opening bid would promise at least a five-card suit. Secondly, when you hold five cards in one suit and four in another, you open in the five-card suit. **Answer:** (b) 1◇.

7.   ♠ A Q 5   ♡ K 7   ◇ A K 10 6   ♣ Q 9 8 2

Since you hold a balanced hand, you should aim to bid notrump as soon as possible. Should you open 1NT? No, because that would show 15-17 HCP and you hold 18 HCP. How about 2NT? No, that would show 20-21 points, so you are not strong enough. You should open one of a suit, intending to rebid 2NT if partner responds at the one-level. With four cards in each minor, you start with 1◇. **Answer:** (b) 1◇.

8.   ♠ A J 8 6   ♡ K 10 8 3   ◇ 7 2   ♣ A J 4

Once again you hold a balanced hand but cannot open 1NT because you do not have 15-17 HCP. Nor can you open 1♠ or 1♡ because these bids promise a five-card suit. You will have to open a three-card minor instead. **Answer:** (a) 1♣.

9.   ♠ 4 2   ♡ A K J 9 3   ◇ 9   ♣ K 10 7 4 2

Always consider your distribution on unbalanced hands. Not only do you have a splendid five-card heart suit, you also have a second five-card suit. Shapely hands like these will provide plenty of tricks if you end as declarer. When you open the bidding on this type of hand do not think: 'I'm being a bit bold, opening on just 11 points'. You have an excellent hand and it would be a big mistake not to open the bidding. With two five-card suits you will open the higher one, as usual. **Answer:** (c) 1♡.

10.   ♠ K   ♡ J 8 7 5 4   ◇ A 10 5 3 2   ♣ Q J

You have 11 HCP and some shape but there are two reasons why you should choose to pass on this hand. Firstly, you would have to open 1♡ and your hearts are weak. You would not want partner to lead a heart if the opponents played in a spade contract. Secondly, if the opponents hold the ace and king, your bare ♣QJ will be worth almost nothing. The same applies to the ♠K. High cards are at their most valuable when they are in your long suits. **Answer:** (a) Pass.

Opening Bid — Problems C

11.   ♠K J 8   ♡A Q   ◇A Q 10 8 3   ♣K Q 9

You pick up this hand (yes, lucky you!). What opening bid will you choose?

     (a) 1◇   (b) 1NT   (c) 2♣   (d) 2NT

12.   ♠Q 9 8 5 4   ♡A J 10 7 6 3   ◇A 10   ♣—

Which action will you select?

     (a) Pass   (b) 1♡   (c) 1♠

                                      23 pts

13.   ♠8   ♡A K J 9 8 2   ◇A K Q 7   ♣A 5

Which of these bids is your choice?

     (a) 1♡   (b) 2♣   (c) 2♡

14.   ♠10 7   ♡A J 5 4 2   ◇A Q 7   ♣A J 8

Which of these bids do you prefer?

     (a) 1♡   (b) 1NT

15.   ♠A J 7 6   ♡A K 5 4   ◇A Q   ♣10 7 6

Which of these bids do you prefer?

     (a) 1♣   (b) 1♡   (c) 1♠   (d) 1NT

(The answers are overleaf.)

Opening Bid — Solutions C

11.   ♠ K J 8   ♡ A Q   ♢ A Q 10 8 3   ♣ K Q 9

You have a balanced hand of 21 HCP. All balanced hands containing 20 or 21 points are opened 2NT, giving an excellent description of your hand immediately. **Answer:** (d) 2NT.

12.   ♠ Q 9 8 5 4   ♡ A J 10 7 6 3   ♢ A 10   ♣ —

Only 11 HCP but remember that to assess the strength of a hand you must look at both the HCP and the shape. With two long major suits and the consequent shortness in the minors, this hand has excellent 'playing strength'. What does that mean? It means that if you end up playing the hand, particularly if partner has a fit for one of your suits, you can expect to make plenty of tricks. As always, you will open in your longer suit, bidding 1♡ rather than 1♠. **Answer:** (b) 1♡.

13.   ♠ 8   ♡ A K J 9 8 2   ♢ A K Q 7   ♣ A 5

Suppose you open 1♡ on this hand and this is followed by three passes. What would your reaction be? You would surely be worried that you had missed a game in hearts! If partner holds as little as three low hearts and no HCP at all, you would have a great chance of scoring at least ten tricks. On hands like these, where you fear missing a game if partner passes a one-bid, you should choose bridge's strongest opening bid: 2♣. Partner will then have to bid, even if he has no points at all. An opening bid of 2♡ would be no good. We will see in a later chapter that this is a weak opening bid, showing a six-card suit and 6-10 points. **Answer:** (b) 2♣.

14.   ♠ 10 7   ♡ A J 5 4 2   ♢ A Q 7   ♣ A J 8

It seems here that you have two satisfactory opening bids: 1♡ and 1NT. Suppose you open 1♡, though, and partner responds 1♠. What will you bid next? It's a problem. You cannot rebid 1NT, showing 12-14 points. Nor should you rebid 2♡. That would suggest a minimum hand with 13-15 points only, and you have a bit more than that. Simply open 1NT, even though you hold a five-card major. **Answer:** (b) 1NT.

15.   ♠ A J 7 6   ♡ A K 5 4   ♢ A Q   ♣ 10 7 6

Opening 1♡ or 1♠ promises at least five cards in your suit, so you cannot do that. 1NT shows 15-17 points and you are too strong for that. You must open 1♣, intending to bid strongly thereafter. If partner responds 1♢, you will jump to 2NT. If partner responds 1♡ or 1♠, you will raise him to the three-level. **Answer:** (a) 1♣.

2

RESPONDING TO ONE OF A SUIT

When your partner opens one of a suit, you know that he holds around 12-19 points, including distribution. When we look at raising partner with a trump fit, we will see that you can add 'support points' because your hand has become more valuable with a trump fit.

If partner opens 1♡ or 1♠, he holds at least five cards in the suit. If instead he opens 1◇ or 1♣ he holds at least three cards in the bid suit and is unlikely to have a five-card major (he would then open in the minor only with six cards or more there). You cannot, at this early stage, tell whether your partner has a minimum opening bid or maybe quite a powerful hand. You will know more when you hear his second bid. For the moment, you must start to describe your own hand.

These are your main options when partner has opened with one of a suit:

- Respond in a new suit at the one-level
- Respond in a new suit at the two-level without jumping
- Respond in notrump
- Raise partner's suit

Responding in a new suit

In general, you need at least 6 points to make a response. If you have fewer points and no particular trump fit, you will pass. To bid a new suit at the one-level requires a suit of at least four cards. Such a response is **forcing**. In other words, your partner must make another bid. Suppose the bidding starts 1◊ — 1♠. Responder may have only 6 points. However, it's also possible that he has 13 points (enough to make a game contract somewhere) or even 18 points (when a slam may be possible). In other words a change-of-suit response is unlimited.

When you have two possible four-card suits in which to respond at the one-level, choose a major suit with a weakish hand (6-9 points) — with 10+ points you can afford to bid your four-card suits up the line since you plan to make more than one bid. With both majors, respond 1♡. A non-jump response in a new suit at the two-level (e.g. 2♣ in response to 1♠) is also unlimited but it shows a minimum of 10 points. You need to be stronger because you are carrying the bidding higher.

When you have two five-card suits, respond in the higher-ranking suit.

When you have one five-card suit and one four-card suit, your response may depend on how many points you hold. Suppose partner opens 1◊ and you have one of these hands:

(1)	♠ A J 7 6	(2)	♠ K Q 8 5
	♡ 8 3		♡ A 6
	◊ 10 4		◊ 10 5
	♣ Q 10 8 7 2		♣ A 10 7 6 4

Hand (1) is fairly weak and worth only one bid. You respond 1♠. You are forced to do this anyway, since your hand is not strong enough for a two-level response in clubs. Hand (2) is strong enough to head for game opposite an opening bid. Since you are worth two bids (at least), you can start with 2♣ intending to bid spades on the next round. Partner will then know that you have at least five clubs and four spades.

Responding in notrump

When you hold 6-9 points and you do not have support for partner's suit, you can either bid a new suit at the one-level or respond 1NT.

When partner opens 1♣ or 1◊ and you hold a balanced 11-12 points with no four-card major, you can respond 2NT. A response of 2NT to an opening bid of 1♡ or 1♠ has a special conventional meaning (Jacoby 2NT) to show a good fit. We will look at that later.

Since game in a minor requires eleven tricks, you will often prefer to play in 3NT even when you have a diamond or club fit. It may prove better to respond 1NT or 2NT rather than raise partner's minor-suit opening.

Although you could respond 3NT with around 13-15 points, it will nearly always work out better to respond in a suit first. This will leave bidding space for partner to tell you more about his hand.

Raising the opener's major suit

When your partner opens 1♡ or 1♠ and you hold trump support (at least 3 cards), you cannot calculate the value of your hand solely in terms of the honors that your hand contains. Because partner may be able to take some ruffs in your hand (the dummy), adding extra tricks to the total, you must allow extra **support points** (also called **dummy points**) for any side-suit shortages. By adding your high-card points to your support points, you can judge how strongly you should bid.

When you have fewer than three cards in a side suit, you can add 'support points'. Shortages become more valuable when you have four-card (or longer) trump support instead of three-card trump support:

Support points

	Three-card support	Four-card support
Doubleton	1	1
Singleton	2	3
Void	3	5

Earlier we mentioned that some people add points for long suits when evaluating opening hands, others add for short suits. However, *everyone* counts support points the same way!

Let's see how shape can add value to the responding hand:

WEST	EAST	WEST	EAST
♠ A K Q 6 5	♠ J 10 7 2	1♠	2♠
♡ J 3	♡ A Q 6 4		
◇ A 10 3	◇ 9 6		
♣ 10 7 6	♣ J 5 3		

West opens 1♠. East has 8 points and a side-suit doubleton (worth an extra 'support point'). It's an 8-point hand, yes, but he thinks of it as being worth 9 points in support of partner's 1♠ bid because the doubleton diamond adds extra value.

Since you need around 10-12 points (allowing for shape) to raise to 3♠, East responds 2♠, ending the auction. The defenders will score three clubs, one diamond and maybe a heart, so you would not want to bid any higher. Note that although you hold four-card support here, you can also raise to 2♠ with only three-card support.

WEST	EAST	WEST	EAST
♠ A K Q 6 5	♠ J 10 7 2	1♠	3♠
♡ J 5	♡ A Q 6 4 3	4♠	
◇ A 10 3	◇ 9		
♣ 10 7 6	♣ J 5 3		

Here East holds the same 8 points but slightly better shape. He holds a side-suit singleton (worth a further 3 support points). With a hand worth 11 points in support of spades, he is minimum for a 3♠ response. Note that a double raise normally promises four-card or longer trump support. Since West has a bit to spare for his opening bid, he advances to 4♠. This is a worthwhile game to bid, since you will make it whenever North holds the ♡K.

When you hold five-card support or better, you are allowed to go all the way to 4♠ on quite a weak hand. This is a form of **preemptive bid**. You bid high because you suspect the opponents have a good fit somewhere and you want to shut them out of the auction. A raise to 4♠ shows at least five-card support and at most 9 HCP.

WEST	EAST	WEST	EAST
♠ A K Q 6 5	♠ J 10 8 7 2	1♠	4♠
♡ J 5	♡ A Q 6 4 3		
◇ A 10 3	◇ 9		
♣ 10 7 6	♣ 8 5		

You can see how well these two hands will play together. You will lose two club tricks and maybe a heart (if South holds the ♡K). The contract is a near certainty.

Since a raise to 4♠ shows this type of hand (sometimes described as a 'weak freak'), you need to make another bid when you are too strong for a double raise and hold four-card support. You begin with an artificial conventional bid, Jacoby 2NT. We will describe this in a moment.

In summary, these are the options with a fit for your partner's 1♠ opening:

2♠	At least three spades, a hand worth 6-9 points in support
2NT	Jacoby 2NT, at least four spades and game values
3♠	at least four spades, worth 10-12 points in support
4♠	at least five spades, at most 9 HCP

With 11+ points and only three-card support, you normally start by responding in a different suit. Eventually, you will want to add splinter bids to your system, so you have an easy way to describe hands with good support for opener and a singleton or void in a side suit, but that discussion is beyond the scope of this book.

Jacoby 2NT

When partner opens 1♡ or 1♠, a response of 2NT shows at least a game raise in partner's suit. It shows trump support of at least four cards. The opener then gives further information about his hand.

Suppose the bidding has started 1♠ - 2NT, the opener can choose from these rebids:

3♣/3◇/3♡	singleton (or void) in the bid suit
3♠	16+ points, no shortage and good trumps
4♣/4◇/4♡	second suit of five or more cards
4♠	minimum opening, no shortage

So, you show a shortage at the three-level and a second five-card suit at the four-level. With a semi-balanced hand (no shortage), you make the strong move of 3♠ with 16+ points. and good trumps, otherwise sign off in 4♠.

Showing your singleton helps responder to judge whether the hands fit well.

WEST	EAST	WEST	EAST
♠ A Q 6 5 3	♠ K 10 8 4	1♠	2NT
♡ A 7 3	♡ K Q 6	3◇	
◇ 3	◇ 10 6 5		
♣ K 9 7 6	♣ A Q 5		

When West announces a singleton diamond, East knows that the hands fit together splendidly. He will head for a slam, which is an excellent contract.

The Jacoby 2NT bidder assesses whether the location of partner's singleton improves his hand or not. His hand improves if he has Axx or xxx (or Axxx or xxxx) opposite the singleton, as East does here. His hand would go downhill if he had a holding such as KJx, since he can only lead up to it once — he may take no tricks at all with those 4 points — they are 'wasted values'.

WEST	EAST	WEST	EAST
♠ A Q 6 5 3	♠ K 10 8 4	1♠	2NT
♡ 3	♡ K Q 6	3♡	4♠
◇ A 7 3	◇ 10 6 5		
♣ K 9 7 6	♣ A Q 5		

Now East has a wasted K-Q combination opposite the singleton. Diagnosing a bad fit between the hands, East signs off in 4♠.

Jacoby 2NT is a most important convention. It is not designed merely to get your side to game — getting to game is a piece of cake with an opening bid facing an opening bid. It is all about getting to slam with perhaps only 26 HCP between you if magic exists, such as a singleton in the right place. How often have you played a hand in 4♠ or 4♡ but made twelve tricks? Turning to partner, you say 'We only had 26 points, but the hands fit really well. I wonder whether we could have bid that?' Well, now you can.

WEST	EAST	WEST	EAST
♠ K Q 8 5 3	♠ A J 9 4	1♠	2NT
♡ 7 5 2	♡ A 10 3	4♠	
◇ K 10 4	◇ Q 8		
♣ A 4	♣ K Q 5 2		

East has some hopes of a slam when he hears partner's opening bid of 1♠. He shows his own strength with the Jacoby 2NT but is turned off by West's announcement of a minimum balanced hand. The partnership stops safely in game.

Responding to one of a suit — Problems A

1. ♠A 10 9 4 ♡9 7 5 ◇Q J 8 2 ♣10 5

Your partner opens 1♣. What will you respond?

    (a) 1◇   (b) 1♠   (c) 1NT

2. ♠9 5 4 ♡Q 10 5 ◇9 3 ♣A Q 10 7 6

Your partner opens 1◇. What will you respond?

    (a) 1NT   (b) 2♣

3. ♠A K 8 4 ♡Q 9 6 5 ◇7 4 ♣Q 9 5

Your partner opens 1◇. What will you respond?

    (a) 1♡   (b) 1♠   (c) 2NT

4. ♠7 ♡A J 5 4 ◇K Q 10 9 6 ♣A 10 5

Partner opens 1♠. Which of these three responses appeals best?

    (a) 2◇   (b) 2♡   (c) 3NT

5. ♠7 ♡K Q 10 6 5 ◇A K 8 7 2 ♣9 6

Partner opens 1♣. What will you respond?

    (a) 1◇   (b) 1♡   (c) 2♡

(The answers are overleaf.)

Responding to one of a suit — Solutions A

1.   ♠ A 10 9 4   ♡ 9 7 5   ◇ Q J 8 2   ♣ 10 5

When partner opens 1♣, you should respond 1♠ (showing a major suit in preference to a minor suit when you are worth only one bid). You should not respond 1NT when you have a major suit to show. **Answer:** (b) 1♠.

2.   ♠ 9 5 4   ♡ Q 10 5   ◇ 9 3   ♣ A Q 10 7 6

Partner opens 1◇. You need at least 10 points to respond at the two-level, so you cannot bid 2♣. Since you have no four-card suit to show at the one-level, you have to respond 1NT. You have a balanced hand here, but 1NT does not necessarily show a balanced hand. **Answer:** (a) 1NT.

3.   ♠ A K 8 4   ♡ Q 9 6 5   ◇ 7 4   ♣ Q 9 5

Partner opens 1◇. You should show a four-card major if you can do so at the one-level. Here you have both majors and should respond in the lower suit, hearts. This will give your partner the chance to rebid in spades if he holds four cards there. **Answer:** (a) 1♡.

4.   ♠ 7   ♡ A J 5 4   ◇ K Q 10 9 6   ♣ A 10 5

Partner opens 1♠. You should respond 2◇, showing your longest suit. If partner holds four or five hearts, he can rebid 2♡ now. Although 3NT may be the best final contract, nothing is lost by responding 2◇ at this stage. You might have a good fit in either diamonds or hearts. Also, a slam may be possible if partner has a strong hand. **Answer:** (a) 2◇.

5.   ♠ 7   ♡ K Q 10 6 5   ◇ A K 8 7 2   ♣ 9 6

Partner opens 1♣. With two five-card suits, you respond in the higher suit, bidding 1♡ instead of 1◇. You will probably have the chance to bid your diamonds on the next round. Although you have enough points to do so, you do not respond at the two-level unless you have to. If partner had opened 1♠ instead, you would have responded 2♡. **Answer:** (b) 1♡.

Responding to one of a suit — Problems B

6.   ♠ 10 2 ♡ K 9 8 3 ◇ 6 5 ♣ A 10 9 8 5

Partner opens 1◇. What will you respond?

    (a) 1♡ .   (b) 1NT   (c) 2♣

7.   ♠ A J 10 4 ♡ 9 7 ◇ A Q 8 6 2 ♣ K 3

Partner opens 1♡. What is your response?

    (a) 1♠   (b) 2◇   (c) 3NT

8.   ♠ A 8 ♡ Q 7 2 ◇ Q 9 7 3 ♣ J 10 7 2

Partner opens 1◇. What will you respond?

    (a) 1NT   (b) 2♣   (c) 2◇   (d) 3◇

9.   ♠ K Q 4 ♡ Q 10 5 ◇ 9 8 2 ♣ K J 8 6

Partner opens 1◇. Which of these three responses looks best?

    (a) 1NT   (b) 2♣   (c) 2NT

10.   ♠ A 10 7 6 ♡ J 9 4 ◇ K 9 7 3 ♣ 10 3

Partner opens 1♡. What response will you make?

    (a) 1♠   (b) 1NT   (c) 2♡

(The answers are overleaf.)

Responding to one of a suit — Solutions B

6.   ♠ 10 2   ♡ K 9 8 3   ◇ 6 5   ♣ A 10 9 8 5

Partner opens 1◇. You should not respond 1NT when you can show a four-card major at the one-level. If you had this shape and 10+ points, you would respond 2♣ with the intention of bidding your hearts on the next round. Since you are not strong enough to bid at the two-level, you should bid 1♡ now. **Answer:** (a) 1♡.

7.   ♠ A J 10 4   ♡ 9 7   ◇ A Q 8 6 2   ♣ K 3

Partner opens 1♡. 3NT may or may not be the right eventual contract but there is no need for you to guess that immediately. To find out more about partner's hand, you should respond in a suit. Since you are strong enough to make two bids (at least), you show your longest suit first. **Answer:** (b) 2◇.

8.   ♠ A 8   ♡ Q 7 2   ◇ Q 9 7 3   ♣ J 10 7 2

Partner opens 1◇. Perhaps you are tempted to raise the diamonds. There are two good reasons why this is not the best idea. Firstly it is possible that partner holds only three diamonds. Secondly, you have stoppers in the other suits and a balanced hand, so 1NT gives a better description of your hand. If partner holds a good hand, the most likely game is 3NT. **Answer:** (a) 1NT.

9.   ♠ K Q 4   ♡ Q 10 5   ◇ 9 8 2   ♣ K J 8 6

Partner opens 1◇. It would not be a mistake to respond 2♣, since you do hold 11 points. However, on hands with no major-suit fit the target game contract is usually 3NT. The bid that gives the best description of your hand is 2NT, showing 11-12 points. You hope that partner can raise to 3NT. **Answer:** (c) 2NT.

10.   ♠ A 10 7 6   ♡ J 9 4   ◇ K 9 7 3   ♣ 10 3

Partner opens 1♡ and therefore has at least five hearts. Since you hold three-card support, you have already found at least an eight-card fit in a major. You are in the 6-9 point range so give partner the good news by raising to 2♡. If you made the mistake of responding 1♠, the bidding might go 1♡ - 1♠; 2♣ - 2♡. Partner would then expect you to hold only two hearts. **Answer:** (c) 2♡.

Responding to one of a suit — Problems C

11.   ♠ K 10 8 3   ♡ K 2   ◇ 8 4   ♣ K 10 8 6 3   9 pts +ss 2 = 11 pts

Partner opens 1♠. How will you respond?

    (a) 2♣   ·(b) 2♠   (c) 3♠

12.   ♠ A K 6   ♡ A 8 2   ◇ 10 9 7 6 2   ♣ 8 3   12

Partner opens 1♡. What response looks best?

    (a) 2◇   (b) 2♡   (c) 3♡

13.   ♠ A Q 8 2   ♡ J 3   ◇ 10 9 4   ♣ A K 7 2

Partner opens 1♠. Which response do you like?

    (a) 2NT (Jacoby)   (b) 3♠   (c) 4♠

14.   ♠ 10 7   ♡ K 10 8 7 2   ◇ Q J 8 7 4   ♣ 6

Partner opens 1♡. How will you respond?

    (a) 2♡   (b) 3♡   (c) 4♡

15.   ♠ 6 4   ♡ A J 8 5 4   ◇ 10 5   ♣ A 8 7 2   9 +ss = 1♥

Partner opens 1♡. How will you respond?

    (a) 2♡   (b) 3♡   (c) 4♡

(The answers are overleaf.)

Responding to one of a suit — Solutions C

11.   ♠K 10 8 3 ♡K 2 ◇8 4 ♣K 10 8 6 3

Partner opens 1♠. With at least a 5-4 fit in spades, it would be pointless to bid your clubs. How high should you raise the spades? You hold 9 HCP and 2 support points for the red-suit doubletons. That is a total of 11 points in support and enough to bid 3♠ rather than 2♠. **Answer:** (c) 3♠.

12.   ♠A K 6 ♡A 8 2 ◇10 9 7 6 2 ♣8 3

Partner opens 1♡. With 11 HCP and an extra support point in clubs, you are too strong to raise to 2♡. Should you bid 3♡? No, because that would promise at least four-card trump support. You should respond 2◇ for the moment. If partner rebids 2♡, showing a fairly minimum hand, you will raise to 3♡. Partner can then decide whether to bid 4♡. **Answer:** (a) 2◇.

13.   ♠A Q 8 2 ♡J 3 ◇10 9 4 ♣A K 7 2

Partner opens 1♠. A response of 3♠ would invite a game and you are too strong for that response. Should you therefore bid 4♠? No, because that is a preemptive response. Your correct bid is 2NT (Jacoby), showing at least game values and four-card spade support. **Answer:** (a) 2NT (Jacoby).

14.   ♠10 7 ♡K 10 8 7 2 ◇Q J 8 7 4 ♣6

Partner opens 1♡. You have a 'weak freak' hand type and should make a preemptive leap to 4♡. Your partner may well make the contract if he has a suitable hand. Meanwhile, your high response may make life difficult for your LHO if his side has a good fit in one of the black suits. **Answer:** (c) 4♡

15.   ♠6 4 ♡A J 8 5 4 ◇10 5 ♣A 8 7 2

Partner opens 1♡. It would not be a mistake to respond 4♡. However, with two aces, your hand is not really suitable for a preemptive response. A more accurate description is a simple limit bid of 3♡. (The reason to bid 4♡ on a weaker and more shapely hand is that if you go down the opponents could probably have made game their way. Here, with two aces in your hand and a partner who has opened the bidding, you do not expect them to make game.) **Answer:** (b) 3♡.

¿w/11 pts = ? how can you go to 4♡?

3

THE OPENER'S REBID

Suppose the bidding starts 1◇ - 1♠. The opener and responder have shown one suit each but little is known about the strength of their hands. The opener might have 12 points or possibly 19 points. The responder holds at least 6 points but might also have closer to 18 points. Neither of them has made a limited bid — a bid that defines their strength within a narrow range.

Suppose instead that the auction starts: 1♠ - 1NT. Now responder has made a limited bid, showing about 6-9 points. As soon as someone makes a limited bid, his partner can take charge of the auction. He will add his strength to partner's and announce the result: partscore, game or game try. Mind you, he can only do that if a satisfactory trump suit has been found or he is happy to play in notrump.

Opener's rebid is a limited bid

The opener has many possible rebids after a start such as 1◇ - 1♠. The following rebids are all limited: 1NT, 2◇, 2♠, 2NT, 3◇, 3♠, 3NT, 4♠. A rebid of 1NT will show 12-14 points since you would have opened 1NT with 15-17. A jump rebid of 2NT shows 18-19 points. A rebid of 3NT shows a powerful hand with long diamonds and sufficient stoppers outside to wish to play in 3NT.

When opener rebids his own suit, 2◇ shows a minimum hand of 12-14 points; 3◇ shows at least six diamonds and 16-18 points. When opener raises partner's spade suit, a rebid of 2♠ shows a minimum hand, and at least three spades to an honor (you can add 'support points' when deciding how high to raise). A raise to 3♠ shows game-try strength (16-18 points); 4♠ shows a powerful hand, enough for game (19-20 points). Raises to the three-level or higher show four-card support.

Opener rebids in a new suit

Another option for the opener is to rebid in a new suit at the cheapest level. Suppose the bidding starts 1♡ - 1♠; 2♣. The opener has shown at least five hearts and four clubs. His strength is still relatively unknown. He might hold 12 points; he might hold 18 points. It will then be the responder's responsibility to look for a limited bid, allowing the opener to judge how high the bidding should go.

A jump rebid in a new suit (1♡ - 1♠; 3♣) is *forcing to game* and therefore shows a very strong hand indeed (19 or more points).

When the first response was at the two-level (promising 10+ points), a new suit bid by the opener (1♡ - 2♣; 2♢) is *forcing for one round*. Consequently, there is no need for the opener to jump to 3♢ to show a strong hand.

Opener 'reverses' in a new suit

Suppose the auction starts 1♢ - 1♠; 2♡. What do you make of the 2♡ rebid? The opener has carried the bidding beyond the safety level of 2♢ (two of the suit in which he opened). This implies that he must hold extra strength, at least 17 points. Such a rebid is known as a **reverse**, and it also promises more cards in the first-bid suit than the second. It is forcing for one round when the response was at the one-level. Opposite a two-level response (1♢ - 2♣; 2♠) a reverse is *forcing to game*. The same is true of a sequence such as 1♡ - 2♢; 3♣, known as a **high reverse.**

When the opener jumps in a new suit opposite a one-level response (1♢ - 1♠; 3♣), this is sometimes called a jump shift. This too is *forcing to game*.

Opener shows strength opposite partner's limited response

When the responder has already made a limited bid, it is the opener's job to announce whether the partnership should stop in a partscore or perhaps bid (or consider) a game contract somewhere.

After a start of 1♠ - 1NT, the opener may 'sign off' (show no game ambition) by passing or rebidding 2♠. He may make a **game try** by bidding 2NT or 3♠. Occasionally he may even bid a game (3NT or 4♠) or offer a choice of games (4♡).

The final option for the opener is to bid a second suit. A minimum rebid in a new suit (2♣, 2♢ or 2♡) is non-forcing. A jump rebid in a new suit is forcing.

Next, suppose the bidding had started 1♠ - 2♠. The responder has shown around 6-9 points and spade support. The opener may hold one of these hands:

(1)	♠ A Q 8 6 5	(2)	♠ A Q J 8 7 2	(3)	♠ A K J 6 5
	♡ 10 9 3		♡ A 7 6		♡ 10 6
	♢ A K 6 3		♢ 8		♢ K 4
	♣ 6		♣ A K 5		♣ A J 8 4

On hand (1) you would pass. Game is not very likely and you would often go down if you strayed above 2♠ on such a hand. With hand (2) you are happy to leap to 4♠; you need very little opposite to have a good chance of ten tricks. Hand (3) is of medium strength and you should make a game try. The best way to help your partner to judge whether to bid 4♠, is to bid your second-longest suit (3♣ here). If partner happens to hold (say) a doubleton club, he will know that you can ruff a club or two in his hand. Ten tricks may then be possible.

The Opener's Rebid — Problems A

1.   ♠ A J 6 ♡ 8 ◇ A J 8 7 3 ♣ K 10 7 6 13 pts

You open 1◇ and partner responds 1♡. What will you rebid?

    (a) 1NT   (b) 2♣   (c) 2◇

2.   ♠ 9 2 ♡ A Q J 7 6 ◇ K J ♣ A K 9 4 18 pts

You open 1♡ and partner responds 1♠. What will you rebid?

    (a) 2♣   (b) 2NT   (c) 3♣

3.   ♠ A J 4 2 ♡ Q 9 7 3 ◇ K 7 ♣ Q J 5 13 pts

You open 1♣ and partner responds 1♡. What will you rebid?

    (a) 1♠   (b) 1NT   (c) 2♡

4.   ♠ Q 3 ♡ A Q 5 4 ◇ A Q 9 8 6 ♣ 8 5 14 pts

You open 1◇ and partner responds 1♠. What will you rebid?

    (a) 1NT   (b) 2◇   (c) 2♡

5.   ♠ A 10 7 2 ♡ 6 ◇ A K J 8 5 3 ♣ A 4 16 pts

You open 1◇ and partner responds 1♡. What will you rebid?

    (a) 1♠   (b) 2◇   (c) 3◇

(The answers are overleaf.)

The Opener's Rebid — Solutions A

1.
♠ A J 6 ♡ 8 ◇ A J 8 7 3 ♣ K 10 7 6

The bidding starts 1◇ - 1♡. A 1NT rebid would show 12-14 points, yes, but it would also tell partner that you held a balanced hand. Here you should rebid 2♣, showing your second suit. It would be a mistake to rebid 2◇, just because you wanted to let partner know that you had a minimum opening bid. **Answer: (b) 2♣.**

2.
♠ 9 2 ♡ A Q J 7 6 ◇ K J ♣ A K 9 4

The bidding starts 1♡ - 1♠. A jump to 2NT would show your 18 points, but showing your second suit with the simple (wide range) rebid of 2♣ describes your hand better. You are not strong enough to rebid 3♣, a 'jump shift'. This would be forcing to game and you cannot justify such an action. Suppose partner holds ♠AQ85 and little else. Game is then very unlikely. **Answer: (a) 2♣.**

3.
♠ A J 4 2 ♡ Q 9 7 3 ◇ K 7 ♣ Q J 5

You have a balanced hand but not enough points to open a 15-17 point 1NT. You open 1♣, intending to rebid 1NT if partner responds 1◇. When partner responds 1♡ instead, you have found an eight-card fit in a major suit and should raise to 2♡. This single raise shows that you are close to a minimum opening bid (around 12-14 points). There would be no purpose in bidding spades when you have already found a satisfactory trump fit. **Answer: (c) 2♡.**

4.
♠ Q 3 ♡ A Q 5 4 ◇ A Q 9 8 6 ♣ 8 5

You open 1◇, partner responding 1♠. It would not be a mistake to rebid 1NT, showing a balanced hand in the 12-14 range. The low doubleton in clubs is a bit worrying, however, and it is better to rebid 2◇. You are not strong enough to rebid 2♡ because this would be a reverse, promising 17 points or more. **Answer: (b) 2◇.**

5.
♠ A 10 7 2 ♡ 6 ◇ A K J 8 5 3 ♣ A 4

You open 1◇, partner responding 1♡. If you were going to rebid in diamonds, you would be worth 3◇ rather than 2◇. However, there is still a chance of finding a spade fit and you should therefore rebid 1♠. You are not nearly strong enough to rebid 2♠, which would be forcing to game. 1♠ is a 'wide-range rebid': you might have 12 points; you might have 18. **Answer: (a) 1♠.**

The Opener's Rebid — Problems B

6.   ♠ A K J 7 6   ♡ A Q 10 4   ◇ J 8   ♣ K 6 *18 pts*

You open 1♠ and partner responds 2◇. What will you rebid?

    (a) 2♡   (b) 3♡   (c) 3NT

7.   ♠ A Q J 7 6 2   ♡ A Q 2   ◇ 10 3   ♣ A 4 *17 pts*

You open 1♠ and partner responds 2◇. What will you rebid?

    (a) 2♠   (b) 3♠   (c) 3NT

8.   ♠ A 10 4   ♡ K Q 4   ◇ A K 10 9 5 4   ♣ Q *18 pts*

You open 1◇ and partner responds 1NT. What will you rebid?

    (a) 2NT   (b) 3◇   (c) 3NT

9.   ♠ 6 3   ♡ A K 9 8 2   ◇ A 8   ♣ A Q 10 7 *17 pts*

You open 1♡ and partner responds 2♣. What will you rebid?

    (a) 3♣   (b) 3♡   (c) 4♣

10.   ♠ A J 7 6 2   ♡ K 10 3   ◇ A 5   ♣ 10 9 3 *12 pts*

You open 1♠ and partner responds 2♣. What will you rebid?

    (a) 2♠   (b) 2NT   (c) 3♣

(The answers are overleaf.)

The Opener's Rebid — Solutions B

6.   ♠A K J 7 6   ♡A Q 10 4   ◇J 8   ♣K 6

The bidding starts 1♠ - 2◇. You should rebid 2♡. Rebidding in a new suit is forcing for one round when partner has responded at the two-level. (This makes good sense. If you had to rebid 3♡ to make sure that partner did not pass, the bidding would be quite high and he would not know whether you held <u>four hearts or five</u>.) You do not yet know whether it will be best to play in spades, hearts, diamonds or notrump. Nor do you know whether a slam is possible. Rebidding 3NT, consuming so much bidding space, would therefore be very unwise. **Answer:** (a) 2♡.

7.   ♠A Q J 7 6 2   ♡A Q 2   ◇10 3   ♣A 4

The bidding starts 1♠ - 2◇. Since you have a good six-card spade suit, you should rebid 3♠. This tells partner of the good suit and the extra high-card strength. **Answer:** (b) 3♠.

8.   ♠A 10 4   ♡K Q 4   ◇A K 10 9 5 4   ♣Q

The bidding starts 1◇ - 1NT. With 18 HCP and a strong six-card diamond suit, you should be able to make 3NT even if partner holds a minimum 6 points. So... bid 3NT! A rebid of either 2NT or 3◇ would be a non-forcing game try and would risk missing an excellent game. **Answer:** (c) 3NT.

9.   ♠6 3   ♡A K 9 8 2   ◇A 8   ♣A Q 10 7

The bidding starts 1♡ - 2♣. You have excellent support for clubs and therefore should agree that suit as trumps. A simple rebid of 3♣ would suggest a hand in the minimum 12-14 point range. Here you should jump to 4♣, to let your partner know that you have a strong hand and want the bidding to go to the game-level (at least). **Answer:** (c) 4♣.

10.   ♠A J 7 6 2   ♡K 10 3   ◇A 5   ♣10 9 3

The bidding starts 1♠ - 2♣. You have already shown a spade suit of five cards or more, so it would not be right to bid that suit again. Partner may hold only four clubs, so it is not attractive to raise to 3♣. The best rebid is 2NT. This is not a jump, so it shows a balanced hand of 12-14 points. Since this is a limited bid, partner will be able to work out whether your side has enough for a game contract. **Answer:** (b) 2NT.

The Opener's Rebid — Problems C

11.   ♠Q 10 4 ♡A K 10 3 ◇8 ♣A K J 7 2 17 pts

You open 1♣ and partner responds 1♠. What will you rebid?

  (a) 2♣   (b) 2♡   (c) 2♠

12.   ♠K Q J 7 2 ♡K 3 ◇A 10 7 3 ♣9 8 13 pts

You open 1♠ and partner responds 2♠. What will you rebid?

  (a) Pass   (b) 3◇   (c) 3♠

13.   ♠K 10 4 ♡A J 9 7 6 4 ◇A 7 3 ♣2 14 pts

You open 1♡ and partner raises to 3♡. What will you rebid?

  (a) Pass   (b) 4♡

14.   ♠K 6 ♡A J 9 2 ◇8 ♣A K 9 8 5 3 17 pts

You open 1♣ and partner responds 1♡. What will you rebid?

  (a) 2♡   (b) 3♡   (c) 4♡

15.   ♠A K J 3 ♡5 ◇Q 5 ♣A K Q 8 7 2 20 pts

You open 1♣ and partner responds 1◇. What will you rebid?

  (a) 1♠   (b) 2♠   (c) 3♣

(The answers are overleaf.)

The Opener's Rebid — Solutions C

11. ♠Q 10 4 ♡A K 10 3 ◇8 ♣A K J 7 2

The bidding starts 1♣ - 1♠. With 17 points, you're strong enough for a reverse to 2♡. This is forcing for one round facing a one-level response. If partner bids spades again, showing five or more cards in the suit, you will have found a satisfactory trump suit and can raise to 4♠. A 2♣ rebid would show a fairly minimum hand and might result in a missed game. Raising spades immediately on three to an honor can be a good idea on a minimum opening bid. You do not have to do it here because you're strong enough for a forcing 2♡. **Answer:** (b) 2♡.

12. ♠K Q J 7 2 ♡K 3 ◇A 10 7 3 ♣9 8

The bidding starts 1♠ - 2♠. Partner has shown a fairly minimum response with at least three spades. Since your hand is close to a minimum, you should pass. **Answer:** (a) Pass.

13. ♠K 10 4 ♡A J 9 7 6 4 ◇A 7 3 ♣2

The bidding starts 1♡ - 3♡. Partner has shown four-card heart support and around 10-12 points, including support points. You should raise to game without thinking twice about it! Although you have only 12 points in high cards, you are entitled to count extra when partner has supported your suit. **Answer:** (b) 4♡.

14. ♠K 6 ♡A J 9 2 ◇8 ♣A K 9 8 5 3

You open 1♣ and partner responds 1♡. You have a splendid hand in support of hearts. Although you have only 15 HCP, you can add one support point for the doubleton spade and three more for the singleton diamond. Your hand is therefore worth 19 points and you should raise to 4♡. **Answer:** (c) 4♡.

15. ♠A K J 3 ♡5 ◇Q 5 ♣A K Q 8 7 2

The bidding starts 1♣ - 1◇. With 19 HCP and fabulous clubs, this is one of those rare hands that justify a forcing-to-game jump rebid in a new suit. Give partner the good news by rebidding 2♠. Although 1♠ would be a wide-range rebid, it would not do justice to your hand. A rebid of 3♣ suffers from two faults: it is non-forcing and does not show your second suit. **Answer:** (b) 2♠.

4

THE RESPONDER'S REBID

Unless the auction starts with bids in three different suits (e.g. 1◊ - 1♠; 2♣), someone will have already made a limited bid by the time responder makes his second call. He will often be in a position to announce the final contract. There are many possibilities and we will handle them in this order.

- The opener rebids in notrump
- The opener rebids his suit
- The opener raises responder's suit
- The opener bids a new suit.

The opener rebids in notrump

When the opener rebids 1NT or 2NT, you will know his strength within a narrow range. You can therefore add your own values and calculate whether a game is possible. You have three general options: sign off, make a game try and bid a game.

Suppose the bidding starts 1◊ - 1♠; 1NT. Your partner has shown 12-14 points with his 1NT rebid. You may have one of these hands:

(1)	♠ A Q 7 6	(2)	♠ K J 10 3	(3)	♠ A Q 10 5 4 2
	♡ 10 6 3		♡ A 7		♡ 7
	◊ 9 4		◊ Q 5 2		◊ J 7 4
	♣ Q 9 6 5		♣ J 10 8 7		♣ A J 3

Hand (1) is fairly weak and you would pass 1NT. Hand (2) is strong enough to invite a game; your two tens may be valuable. You rebid 2NT, allowing partner to advance to 3NT when he is in the upper half of his 12-14 range. Hand (3) is worth a jump to 4♠ facing a balanced minimum opening bid.

The opener rebids his suit

Suppose the bidding starts 1◇ - 1♠; 2◇. Partner has suggested a minimum hand (usually 12-14 points). He will probably hold six diamonds, since he has not bid another suit, rebid in notrump or raised your suit. As responder, what would you do next on these hands?

(4)	♠ K Q 8 7 2	(5)	♠ A Q 8 7	(6)	♠ A Q 10 5 4
	♡ K 7 3		♡ K 10 3		♡ K J 7 2
	◇ 9		◇ 10 4		◇ K 5
	♣ J 8 4 2		♣ Q 9 7 2		♣ 10 6

Hand (4) is weak and offers no prospect of game. You should pass. Do not make another bid simply because you 'do not like diamonds'. On hand (5), with 11 points and stoppers in the unbid suits (hearts and clubs) you will make a game try of 2NT. Partner can then choose between passing or, with a better hand, raising to 3NT. On hand (6) you have enough to merit a game contract. You are not yet sure which game will be best. You should rebid 2♡. *A bid in a new suit is forcing* after partner has rebid his suit.

You have similar options when partner has shown a better hand with a jump rebid in his suit. Perhaps the bidding has started 1♡ - 1♠; 3♡ and you hold one of these hands:

(7)	♠ K Q 8 2	(8)	♠ K 10 7 6 2	(9)	♠ A K 10 8 3 2
	♡ 7 4		♡ 8		♡ 7
	◇ A J 9 3		◇ Q 10 8 5		◇ A 8 5
	♣ 10 5 4		♣ Q 9 3		♣ 6 4 3

Partner will have around 16-18 points and a six-card heart suit. You should raise to 4♡ on hand (7). It's quite okay to support with two trumps when your partner has shown a suit of at least six cards. On hand (8), with only 7 points and a singleton in partner's suit, you should simply pass. Do not bid 3♠ or 3NT because 'I didn't like your hearts, partner'. A good general rule is to bid high when you have a trump fit and to keep low when there is a misfit.

You have enough for game on hand (9) but you are not sure which game will be best. You should rebid 3♠, which is forcing after a jump rebid by the opener.

The opener raises responder's suit

When the bidding starts 1♣ - 1♠; 2♠ or 1◇ - 1♡; 3♡, the opener not only shows support for responder's suit, he also limits the strength of his hand. The higher he bids, the stronger he is. The responder will add his strength to that indicated by the opener and decide whether to pass, make a game try or bid game.

Suppose you are the responder and the bidding starts 1◇ - 1♠; 2♠. You must find a rebid on each of these hands:

(10) ♠ K J 8 2   (11) ♠ A K 9 4   (12) ♠ A J 9 5 4
     ♡ A 10 7   ♡ K 4   ♡ A 9 7 2
     ◇ 9   ◇ J 4 2   ◇ 10 5
     ♣ 10 8 4 3 2   ♣ 10 8 6 5   ♣ K 5

On hand (10) you should pass. You have only 8 points facing partner's 12-14. The singleton is not a bonus when it lies opposite partner's bid suit.

Hand (11) is stronger and worth a game try. Since you have only four spades and partner will occasionally raise to 2♠ on a hand with only three-card support, you should bid 2NT rather than 3♠.

With hand (12) you are very happy to bid 4♠. Not only do you hold 12 points, you have a precious fifth trump.

The opener bids a new suit

When the bidding starts 1♡ - 1♠; 2♣, the opener has not really limited his hand. He will hold somewhere between 12 and 18 points. Responder may pass, although he will be reluctant to do this when his values might be enough for game when the opener is close to maximum. These are the main options for responder:

Sign off on weak hand (6-9 points)

Pass	Weak hand, prefers clubs to hearts
2♡	Preference for hearts, often with only two hearts
2♠	Around 6-9 points with six spades

Try for game on medium hand (10-12 points)

2NT	11-12 points, game try with stopper(s) in diamonds
3♣	9-11 points with at least four-card club support
3♡	Jump preference for hearts, 10-11 points, three-card support
3♠	6+ spades, 10-11 points

Game values (13+ points)

2◇	Fourth suit forcing, an artificial bid on a strong hand (see Chapter 12)
3NT/4♡/4♠	When you know which game will be best

Let's say that the bidding has started 1♡ - 1♠; 2♣ and as responder you have to find a next move on one of these hands:

(13) ♠ A J 9 8 2   (14) ♠ A 10 9 3   (14) ♠ K 9 8 6
     ♡ 10 7   ♡ 5 4   ♡ 8 4
     ◇ Q 10 9 3   ◇ K J 9 6   ◇ A K 9 2
     ♣ 9 3   ♣ Q J 5   ♣ K 10 5

On hand (13) you are not strong enough to rebid 2NT. This would show around 11-12 points and invite a game. Instead you should bid 2♡. You are 'giving preference' between partner's suits. Such a bid does not show heart support; it merely says that 2♡ may be the best contract available. Indeed, if you held three hearts and only 6-9 points you would have raised to 2♡ on the first round, rather than responding 1♠. Rebidding 2♠ would be a mistake and might leave you in a 5-1 fit. In hearts you know that you have at least a 5-2 fit.

Hand (14) is stronger and you should make a game try of 2NT.

On hand (15) you have no intention of stopping in a partscore; with handsome diamond stoppers you are happy to jump to 3NT.

Sometimes the responder is strong enough for game but cannot yet tell which game will be best. In that case he can use a popular and very useful convention, 'fourth suit forcing'. We will look at this in Chapter 12.

We will end by looking at the situation where the opener has reversed, rebidding a new suit at a higher level than two of his first suit. Such an action shows extra values and you must allow for this when deciding how high to bid as responder.

The bidding starts 1◇ - 1♠; 2♡ and as responder you hold:

(16) ♠ Q J 7 2   (17) ♠ K J 9 7   (18) ♠ A K 9 5
     ♡ 10 7 5   ♡ J 4   ♡ Q 7
     ◇ K 4   ◇ Q 7 6   ◇ A J 9 2
     ♣ A 10 9 3   ♣ 10 8 6 3   ♣ J 10 5

On hand (16) you have 10 points opposite a reverse and this is enough for game. With a robust A1093 in the unbid club suit, you are very happy to leap to 3NT. On hand (17) the clubs are not strong enough to bid notrump. You will bid a simple 3◇ and leave any further move to partner. On hand (18) you have a feeling that a slam in diamonds may be possible. You should bid 4◇, telling partner that you have a good hand with strong diamond support.

The Responder's Rebid — Problems A

1.   ♠ A 9 4   ♡ K Q 7 6   ◇ J 8 2   ♣ 10 5 3

The bidding starts 1◇ - 1♡; 1NT. What will you say now as responder?

     (a) Pass   (b) 2◇   (c) 2NT

2.   ♠ K 8 7 6 3   ♡ J 10 5   ◇ Q 3   ♣ J 9 8

The bidding starts 1◇ - 1♠; 2NT. What will you say now as responder?

     (a) Pass   (b) 3♠   (c) 3NT

3.   ♠ 7 4   ♡ J 9 8 2   ◇ K 3   ♣ A Q 10 5 2

The bidding starts 1♠ - 2♣; 2NT. What will you bid now?

     (a) Pass   (b) 3♡   (c) 3NT

4.   ♠ A K 10 8 7 2   ♡ K 10 8   ◇ 10 6   ♣ 5 4

The bidding starts 1♣ - 1♠; 2♣. What will you bid next, as responder?

     (a) 2♠   (b) 3♠   (c) 4♠

5.   ♠ 8 2   ♡ A Q 6   ◇ J 8 4   ♣ K 10 7 5 3

The bidding starts 1♣ - 3♣; 3◇. What will you say next?

     (a) 3♡   (b) 3NT   (c) 4♣   (d) 5♣

(The answers are overleaf.)

The Responder's Rebid — Solutions A

1.   ♠A 9 4 ♡K Q 7 6 ◇J 8 2 ♣10 5 3

The bidding starts 1◇ - 1♡; 1NT. With only 10 points opposite 12-14, you are not strong enough to try for game. (With two balanced hands, you need a combined 25 points for 3NT.) You should pass. **Answer:** (a) Pass.

2.   ♠K 8 7 6 3 ♡J 10 5 ◇Q 3 ♣J 9 8

The bidding starts 1◇ - 1♠; 2NT. Partner has shown a balanced hand containing 18-19 points. Add your 7 points and you have enough for game. You should raise to 3NT. There is not much point in bidding the spades again, just in case you have a 5-3 fit there. If partner holds three spades, you should be able to make four or five spade tricks in 3NT. **Answer:** (c) 3NT.

3.   ♠7 4 ♡J 9 8 2 ◇K 3 ♣A Q 10 5 2

The bidding starts 1♠ - 2♣; 2NT. Partner has shown 12-14 points, so you cannot raise to game on just 10 points. You might have only 22 points between you! You should pass. Suppose you held ♡K982 instead. The combined point-count would then be 24-26 and you would raise to 3NT. **Answer:** (a) Pass.

4.   ♠A K 10 8 7 2 ♡K 10 8 ◇10 6 ♣5 4

After a start of 1♣ - 1♠; 2♣, you must consider your next move. You are too strong for 2♠, which would be a sign-off. With about 11 points and a good six-card suit, your hand is just right for 3♠. Going all the way to game would be a stretch, particularly as partner might hold only one spade or none at all. **Answer:** (b) 3♠.

5.   ♠8 2 ♡A Q 6 ◇J 8 4 ♣K 10 7 5 3

After a start of 1♣ - 3♣ your partner rebids 3◇. What does this mean? You have already found a club fit, so he cannot be suggesting diamonds as trumps. He is showing you a diamond **stopper** (perhaps ◇AK7) in the hope that a final contract of 3NT may be possible. Since he did not bid 3NT himself, he probably has no stopper in one of the major suits and is hoping that you can help. You should rebid 3♡ to announce that you have a heart stopper. He may then be happy to bid 3NT. You can see how much better this sort of bidding is than simply bidding 3NT in the hope that every suit is stopped. **Answer:** (a) 3♡.

The Responder's Rebid — Problems B

6.   ♠9 4 2 ♡K J 7 6 ◇8 7 3 ♣A Q 6

The bidding starts 1◇ - 1♡; 2♡. What will you say now as responder?

    (a) Pass   (b) 2NT   (c) 3♡

7.   ♠J 8 7 4 ♡Q 9 8 2 ◇K 3 2 ♣10 5

The bidding starts 1♣ - 1♡; 3♡. What will you say now as responder?

    (a) Pass   (b) 3NT   (c) 4♡

8.   ♠6 2 ♡K 5 2 ◇Q 10 4 ♣A K J 6 4

The bidding starts 1♠ - 2♣; 3♣. What will you bid now?

    (a) 3◇   (b) 3NT   (c) 4♣   (d) 5♣

9.   ♠A K 8 3 2 ♡A 10 3 ◇K 6 4 ♣5 4

The bidding starts 1♣ - 1♠; 4♠. What will you bid next, as responder?

    (a) Pass   (b) 4NT   (c) 5♠   (d) 6♠

10.   ♠9 8 4 ♡A Q 6 ◇A J 8 4 ♣8 7 5

The bidding starts 1◇ - 3◇; 3♠. What will you say next?

    (a) 3NT   (b) 4◇   (c) 5◇

(The answers are overleaf.)

The Responder's Rebid — Solutions B

6.   ♠9 4 2 ♡K J 7 6 ◇8 7 3 ♣A Q 6

The bidding starts 1◇ - 1♡; 2♡. Partner has shows a minimum hand of around 12-14 points. With 10 points and 4-3-3-3 shape, you are not quite strong enough to make a game try and should pass. **Answer:** (a) Pass.

7.   ♠J 8 7 4 ♡Q 9 8 2 ◇K 3 2 ♣10 5

The bidding starts 1♣ - 1♡; 3♡. Partner has shown better than a minimum, but not enough for game. He will have 16-18 points (perhaps including some 'support points'). Your hand represents a minimum response. You have nothing extra for your bidding so far and should pass. **Answer:** (a) Pass.

8.   ♠6 2 ♡K 5 2 ◇Q 10 4 ♣A K J 6 4

The bidding starts 1♠ - 2♣; 3♣. Partner has shown around 12-14 points and you are strong enough to head for game. When you have a fit in a minor suit, it is usually right to play in 3NT rather than five of a minor. You will then need to score only nine tricks instead of eleven. Here you have stoppers in both the red suits and therefore an easy rebid of 3NT. **Answer:** (b) 3NT.

9.   ♠A K 8 3 2 ♡A 10 3 ◇K 6 4 ♣5 4

After a start of 1♣ - 1♠; 4♠, it would be a huge mistake to pass. By raising all the way to game when you might have held just 6 points, partner has shown a great hand (19 or 20 points). You can surely make a slam and should 'ask for aces' with 4NT (we will look at the Blackwood 4NT bid in Chapter 13). **Answer:** (b) 4NT.

10.   ♠9 8 4 ♡A Q 6 ◇A J 8 4 ♣8 7 5

What does partner's 3♠ mean in the sequence 1◇ - 3◇; 3♠? It is a **stopper bid**. He is hoping for a 3NT contract but cannot bid it himself because he has no stopper in hearts. (Doubtless he has a club stopper or it's unlikely that he would be heading for game.) Since you hold a healthy ♡AQ6, you are happy to bid 3NT. **Answer:** (a) 3NT.

The Responder's Rebid — Problems C

11.   ♠ K Q 6 4   ♡ K J 3   ◇ Q 8 2   ♣ 10 9 5

The bidding starts 1◇ - 1♠; 2♣. As responder, what is your next bid?

     (a) 2◇   (b) 2NT   (c) 3◇   (d) 3NT

12.   ♠ Q J 7 6   ♡ Q 9 2   ◇ K 10 8 4   ♣ K 5

The bidding starts 1♡ - 1♠; 2◇. As responder, what is your next bid?

     (a) 2NT   (b) 3◇   (c) 3♡   (d) 4♡

13.   ♠ 8 3 2   ♡ A 6 4   ◇ A Q 10 9 7   ♣ 10 2

The bidding starts 1♠ - 2◇; 2♡. What is your next action?

     (a) Pass   (b) 2♠   (c) 3◇   (d) 3♡

14.   ♠ A 10 9 7 6   ♡ K J 7 3   ◇ 8 5   ♣ 10 9

The bidding starts 1◇ - 1♠; 2♣. What now?

     (a) Pass   (b) 2◇   (c) 2♡   (d) 2♠   (e) 2NT

15.   ♠ 7 2   ♡ A 8 2   ◇ K J 4   ♣ A 10 8 7 2

The bidding starts 1♡ - 2♣; 2♠. How will you continue?

     (a) 2NT   (b) 3♡   (c) 3NT   (d) 4♡

(The answers are overleaf.)

The Responder's Rebid — Solutions C

11.   ♠KQ64   ♡KJ3   ◇Q82   ♣1095

The bidding starts 1◇ - 1♠; 2♣. It's your task to make the first limit bid. Bidding 2◇ would not be enough with 11 points. A jump to 3◇ would be a better description but the most constructive rebid is 2NT, suggesting 11-12 HCP and a stopper in hearts, the unbid suit. This is a non-forcing limit bid. Partner is entitled to pass with nothing to spare for the opening bid. **Answer:** (b) 2NT.

12.   ♠QJ76   ♡Q92   ◇K1084   ♣K5

The bidding starts 1♡ - 1♠; 2◇. You are too strong to sign off and not strong enough to insist on game. You should make a game try, leaving the final decision to your partner. You have good support for both hearts and diamonds, but you should bid 3♡, showing your fit in the major. Eleven tricks is a tough target, so bidding game in a minor suit is something you should seek to avoid. **Answer:** (c) 3♡.

13.   ♠832   ♡A64   ◇AQ1097   ♣102

The bidding starts 1♠ - 2◇; 2♡. You have three-card support for partner's spades, so you need to show it now. However, to show that you have only minimum values for responding at the two-level, you should bid just 2♠ at your second turn. Jumping to 3♠ would show a game-forcing hand. **Answer:** (b) 2♠.

14.   ♠A10976   ♡KJ73   ◇85   ♣109

The start is 1◇ - 1♠; 2♣. You have a good stopper in hearts but 8 points is not enough to justify a game try of 2NT. Your spades are not strong enough for 2♠; partner might well hold only one spade. On hands such as this, you display your lack of ambition by giving preference to 2◇. Partner probably holds five diamonds and four clubs, so it would be a poor idea to pass instead of bidding 2◇. Bidding 2♡ would be game-forcing (see Chapter 12). **Answer:** (b) 2◇.

15.   ♠72   ♡A82   ◇KJ4   ♣A10872

Partner shows extra values with a reverse: 1♡ - 2♣; 2♠. This is forcing to game facing a two-level response. (The points will be 17 opposite 10 at least, so this makes good sense.) With three-card support for partner's longer major, you should not think of bidding notrump. You should bid 3♡. Remember that the bidding must go to the game-level at least. By bidding 3♡ instead of the space-consuming 4♡, you allow partner the chance to investigate a possible slam. **Answer:** (b) 3♡.

5

COMPLETING THE AUCTION

The first four bids by you and your partner lay the foundation stones of a good auction. We will now see how auctions of five bids or more are brought to a close by the opener. (We will look at slam auctions in Chapters 13 and 14.)

The responder has signed off

When the responder signs off at his second turn, showing a weak hand, this is not necessarily the end of the auction. When the opener is strong, he can either bid a game somewhere or make a game try.

Suppose the bidding starts 1♡ - 1♠; 2♣ - 2♡. Your partner has shown around 6-9 points and a doubleton heart. (If he had three-card heart support and a minimum response, he would have raised to 2♡ at his first turn.) What should you say now on these three hands?

(1)	♠ 6	(2)	♠ K 3	(3)	♠ Q 10 5
	♡ A K 9 7 6		♡ A Q 10 9 5		♡ A K 8 7 2
	◇ J 7 3		◇ A J		◇ 4
	♣ A K 6 5		♣ K 10 7 2		♣ A Q 10 3

Hand (1) has some extra strength but not enough to bid again. Remember that the heart fit (if we can call it that) is likely to be only 5-2. Nor is the singleton spade a welcome feature when partner has bid the suit.

Hand (2) contains 17 points. The ◇AJ may represent a double stopper if partner holds the ◇Q or perhaps ◇10xx. You are worth a game try of 2NT.

On hand (3) there is a chance of game if partner has a five-card spade suit. You should continue with 2♠. If partner advances to 3♠, which he may do when holding five spades, you will bid 4♠.

The responder has made a game try

When the responder's second bid is a game try, you may have two decisions to make: whether to advance at all and choosing the best denomination.

Suppose the bidding starts 1♡ - 2♣; 2♡ - 2NT. Partner has shown 11-12 HCP with stoppers in the unbid suits. How will you continue on these opening hands?

(4)	♠ K 7	(5)	♠ K 10 4	(6)	♠ A 4
	♡ K J 9 8 6 5		♡ A Q 9 8 7 4 2		♡ A K 7 6 4 2
	◇ A 8 3		◇ Q 4		◇ K 5
	♣ J 8		♣ 7		♣ 10 6 3

Hand (4) is nothing special. You have already bid the hearts twice and partner has shown no interest in the suit. You should pass 2NT.

Hand (5) has a seven-card heart suit but is otherwise pretty minimal. You should bid 3♡. If partner thinks he can make game opposite 11 or 12 HCP and a seven-card heart suit, he can raise to 4♡.

Hand (6) contains 14 HCP and you will raise to 3NT.

The responder has bid game

When you have not yet limited your hand as opener and partner bids game at his second turn, the bidding is not necessarily over. If you have a strong hand, you may see possibilities of a slam.

Suppose you are the opener and the bidding starts 1◇ - 1♠; 2♣ - 3NT. What action, if any, is appropriate on these hands?

(7)	♠ 3	(8)	♠ J 5	(9)	♠ 4
	♡ K 4		♡ Q 4		♡ A 9
	◇ A K 10 9 6		◇ A Q J 10 4		◇ A K J 7 6 2
	♣ A Q J 7 3		♣ A K J 7		♣ A Q 6 5

Hand (7) is very powerful if you can find a trump fit. You should rebid 4♣, showing your fifth card in the club suit. If partner has no interest in either minor suit, he is allowed to sign off in 4NT. (A bid of 4NT often asks for aces, or keycards, as we will see in Chapters 13 and 14, but that is only after a trump suit has been agreed.)

Hand (8) has 18 HCP. You expect partner to have around 13-15 points. Here you are entitled to raise 3NT to 4NT, inviting a slam. Again, 4NT does not ask for aces.

On hand (9) the chances are surely good for a diamond slam. You should continue to 4◇, showing a strong hand with an excellent diamond suit.

Completing the Auction — Problems A

1. ♠ A K 4 ♡ 6 ◇ A J 8 7 2 ♣ K Q 9 3

The bidding starts 1◇ - 1♡; 2♣ - 2◇. What will you say now as the opener?

   (a) Pass   (b) 2NT   (c) 3◇

2. ♠ K 8 7 ♡ A Q 9 4 2 ◇ K Q 6 5 ♣ 7

The bidding starts 1♡ - 1♠; 2◇ - 2NT. What will you say now as the opener?

   (a) Pass   (b) 3♠   (c) 3NT

3. ♠ 4 ♡ Q 9 7 ◇ A K 9 8 6 5 ♣ A J 7

The bidding starts 1◇ - 1♠; 2◇ - 2♠. What will you bid now?

   (a) Pass   (b) 2NT   (c) 3◇

4. ♠ J 8 7 ♡ Q 8 ◇ A K J 9 7 5 ♣ K 10

The bidding starts 1◇ - 1♠; 2◇ - 2♡. What will you bid next?

   (a) 2♠   (b) 3◇   (c) 3♠

5. ♠ A Q 10 6 ♡ A 6 ◇ 10 ♣ A K J 8 7 2

The bidding starts 1♣ - 1◇; 1♠ - 3NT. What will you say next?

   (a) Pass   (b) 4♣   (c) 6NT

(The answers are overleaf.)

Completing the Auction — Solutions A

1. ♠ A K 4 ♡ 6 ◇ A J 8 7 2 ♣ K Q 9 3

The bidding starts 1◇ - 1♡; 2♣ - 2◇. With 17 points and a double stopper in spades, you are entitled to make a game try of 2NT. 3◇ would not be such an accurate advance. Not only would you keep partner in the dark about your good spade stopper, you might have only a 5-2 fit in diamonds. **Answer:** (b) 2NT.

2. ♠ K 8 7 ♡ A Q 9 4 2 ◇ K Q 6 5 ♣ 7

The bidding starts 1♡ - 1♠; 2◇ - 2NT. With 14 points opposite partner's 11-12, you have enough to bid game. In case partner holds five spades, you should bid 3♠ now. This is forcing. It could not logically be otherwise, since partner will have to bid 3NT anyway if he holds only four spades. **Answer:** (b) 3♠.

3. ♠ 4 ♡ Q 9 7 ◇ A K 9 8 6 5 ♣ A J 7

The bidding starts 1◇ - 1♠; 2◇ - 2♠. Partner has around 6-9 points and a six-card spade suit. You should pass. You are not strong enough to invite a game with 2NT. You have already shown long diamonds and it would be very unwise to bid the suit again. For one thing, this would raise the auction to the three-level. Get out as low as you can when you have a **misfit**. **Answer:** (a) Pass.

4. ♠ J 8 7 ♡ Q 8 ◇ A K J 9 7 5 ♣ K 10

After a start of 1◇ - 1♠; 2◇ - 2♡, you must consider your next move. Partner's sequence is forcing, so he is likely to hold at least 10 points. So far, he has shown five spades and four hearts (with four spades and four hearts, his first response would have been 1♡). You are too strong to give mere preference to 2♠ and should jump to 3♠. **Answer:** (c) 3♠.

5. ♠ A Q 10 6 ♡ A 6 ◇ 10 ♣ A K J 8 7 2

The bidding starts 1♣ - 1◇; 1♠ - 3NT. It would not be wrong to bid 6NT, but a slam could be better in clubs if partner has a fit for that suit. You should show the good clubs by bidding 4♣. An advance from the game contract of 3NT into four of a minor is forcing and shows a very good hand. **Answer:** (b) 4♣.

Completing the Auction — Problems B

6.   ♠ 10 8 3   ♡ 6   ◇ A Q 8   ♣ A K 10 8 6 5

The bidding starts 1♣ - 1♡; 2♣ - 3♣. What will you say now as the opener?

      (a) Pass   (b) 3◇   (c) 5♣

7.   ♠ K Q 7 3   ♡ 2   ◇ K Q J 8 2   ♣ A 10 8

The bidding starts 1◇ - 1♡; 1♠ - 2♠. What will you say now as the opener?

      (a) Pass   (b) 3♣   (c) 3♠

8.   ♠ A Q 8 7 2   ♡ A Q   ◇ 6 5   ♣ Q 10 8 3

The bidding starts 1♠ - 1NT; 2♣ - 2◇. What will you bid now?

      (a) Pass   (b) 2♠   (c) 2NT

9.   ♠ A Q J 8 5 2   ♡ Q 7   ◇ J 9 7   ♣ K 3

The bidding starts 1♠ - 2♡; 2♠ - 3♣. What will you bid next?

      (a) 3♡   (b) 3♠   (c) 3NT

10.   ♠ K Q 6   ♡ 7 6   ◇ J 8   ♣ K Q J 7 6 2

The bidding starts 1♣ - 1♡; 2♣ - 3♡. What will you say next?

      (a) Pass   (b) 3♠   (c) 3NT   (d) 4♡

(The answers are overleaf.)

Completing the Auction — Solutions B

6.   ♠ 10 8 3 ♡ 6 ♢ A Q 8 ♣ A K 10 8 6 5

The bidding starts 1♣ - 1♡; 2♣ - 3♣. Partner has raised the clubs. This is a non-forcing limit bid, showing 10-12 points. You are worth accepting the try with six good clubs and a side ace-queen. The best continuation is 3♢. When a minor suit has been agreed, a new suit at the three-level shows a stopper. Here you hope that partner has a spade stopper and can bid 3NT. If not, you are likely to end in 5♣. **Answer:** (b) 3♢.

7.   ♠ K Q 7 3 ♡ 2 ♢ K Q J 8 2 ♣ A 10 8

The bidding starts 1♢ - 1♡; 1♠ - 2♠. Partner has four-card spade support and fewer than 10 points. What is your hand worth? The singleton heart is not as good as it may seem because partner has bid that suit. Nevertheless, there might easily be a playable game available. You are worth a game try of 3♣. Partner will realize that you are very short in hearts and value his hand accordingly. **Answer:** (b) 3♣.

8.   ♠ A Q 8 7 2 ♡ A Q ♢ 6 5 ♣ Q 10 8 3

The bidding starts 1♠ - 1NT; 2♣ - 2♢. Partner is weak with long diamonds. If he held 10 points or more, he would have responded 2♢ and not 1NT. You are not strong enough to invite a game with 2NT and should pass. You have already shown five spades, so there is no reason to bid the spades again. **Answer:** (a) Pass.

9.   ♠ A Q J 8 5 2 ♡ Q 7 ♢ J 9 7 ♣ K 3

After a start of 1♠ - 2♡; 2♠ - 3♣, you must consider your next move. Partner's 2♡ response showed at least five hearts. His rebid in a new suit is forcing to game. You have already bid your spades twice and your diamonds are not good enough to bid 3NT. You should bid 3♡ in case partner holds six hearts. He will not expect three-card support since you did not raise hearts on the previous round. **Answer:** (a) 3♡.

10.   ♠ K Q 6 ♡ 7 6 ♢ J 8 ♣ K Q J 7 6 2

The bidding starts 1♣ - 1♡; 2♣ - 3♡. Partner has made a game try on a hand that contains six hearts. Since you hold a minimum opener, you should pass. The doubleton heart would be sufficient support to raise to 4♡ if you held a few more points. **Answer:** (a) Pass.

Completing the Auction — Problems C

11.   ♠4   ♡Q96   ◇AQ974   ♣AKJ4

The bidding starts 1◇ - 1♡; 2♣ - 2NT. What will you say now as the opener?

   (a) Pass   (b) 3◇   (c) 3♡   (d) 3NT

12.   ♠K8   ♡1073   ◇K5   ♣AKJ1076

The bidding starts 1♣ - 1♠; 2♣ - 3♠. What will you say now as the opener?

   (a) Pass   (b) 3NT   (c) 4♣   (d) 4♠

13.   ♠10   ♡AQ1073   ◇AJ2   ♣AK74

The bidding starts 1♡ - 1♠; 2♣ - 2♡. What will you bid now?

   (a) 2NT   (b) 3♡   (c) 3NT   (d) 4♡

14.   ♠AQJ872   ♡97   ◇A4   ♣KQ4

The bidding starts 1♠ - 1NT; 3♠ - 3NT. What will you bid next?

   (a) Pass   (b) 4♠

15.   ♠AQ6   ♡KQ1095   ◇AQ8   ♣J7

The bidding starts 1♡ - 1NT; 2NT - 3♣. What will you say next?

   (a) Pass   (b) 3♡   (c) 3NT

(The answers are overleaf.)

Completing the Auction — Solutions C

11.   ♠4 ♡Q96 ◇AQ974 ♣AKJ4

The bidding starts 1◇ - 1♡; 2♣ - 2NT. Partner has around 11 points and is inviting a game. With 16 points, you are easily strong enough to accept. However, if partner holds five hearts it may well be better to play in 4♡ rather than 3NT. You should bid 3♡ to show your three-card heart support now. This is forcing to game. If instead you held only 12 points and this shape, you would pass 2NT. (You might well have raised to 2♡ at your second turn with such a hand.) **Answer:** (c) 3♡.

12.   ♠K8 ♡1073 ◇K5 ♣AKJ1076

The bidding starts 1♣ - 1♠; 2♣ - 3♠. Partner holds six spades and game-invitational values, perhaps 10 or 11 points. You have a good hand in support of spades (a high trump honor, a good club side suit, a possible ruffing value in diamonds and 14 HCP). You are easily worth a raise to 4♠. **Answer:** (d) 4♠.

13.   ♠10 ♡AQ1073 ◇AJ2 ♣AK74

The bidding starts 1♡ - 1♠; 2♣ - 2♡. Partner has signed off on a hand with around 6-9 points. He almost certainly has only two hearts, since with three hearts he would have raised to 2♡ instead of showing his spades. You are entitled to make a game try with 18 HCP in your hand. Since the heart fit is likely to be 5-2, you should bid 2NT to invite a game in notrump. **Answer:** (a) 2NT.

14.   ♠AQJ872 ♡97 ◇A4 ♣KQ4

After a start of 1♠ - 1NT; 3♠ - 3NT, you have already described your hand admirably. Bidding 4♠ might make partner think that you did not trust him. Remember that his 1NT response did not guarantee a balanced hand. He may well hold only one spade and might even be void in the suit. Whatever he has, you know that he thinks that 3NT will be a better prospect than 4♠ and you have no reason to overrule that decision. **Answer:** (a) Pass.

15.   ♠AQ6 ♡KQ1095 ◇AQ8 ♣J7

The bidding starts 1♡ - 1NT; 2NT - 3♣. As on the previous example, you have already described your hand perfectly: you have a balanced hand of around 18 HCP. If partner thought that 3NT would be a good idea, that is what he would have bid! He is telling you that he thinks 3♣ will be a safer contract than 2NT. He will have a minimum response with six or seven weakish clubs. **Answer:** (a) Pass.

6

RESPONDING TO 1NT

One of the best starts to an auction is a 1NT opening. With just one bid, you paint a clear picture of your hand. Most of the time the responder will know immediately whether to limit his ambitions to a partscore or head towards a game or slam.

These are the main responses available to you when partner has opened 1NT:

2♣	Stayman convention, asking partner to show a four-card major
2♦	Transfer response, shows 5+ hearts and asks partner to bid 2♥
2♥	Transfer response, shows 5+ spades and asks partner to bid 2♠
2NT	Shows 8-9 points and invites partner to bid 3NT
3♣/3♦/3♥/3♠	Slam try, with 6+ cards in the bid suit (not everyone plays this way)
3NT	10+ points, no interest in the major suits

Transfer responses can be made on hands of any strength. Partner is going to bid again and you will then have the opportunity to show how strong you are.

The responder signs off

When your responding hand is fairly weak and you wish to play in a partscore, you may either pass the 1NT opening bid or transfer into a major suit of at least five cards. Suppose your partner has opened 1NT, and the next player passes:

(1)	♠ 6 3	(2)	♠ J 10 7	(3)	♠ 9 8 2
	♡ A J 9 6		♡ Q 10 8 7 3		♡ Q 6
	♦ 10 8 4		♦ 9 8 4		♦ K 9 8 6 5
	♣ Q 8 6 5		♣ K 4		♣ 10 7 3

If partner had opened with one of a suit (which covers a wide range of about 12-19 points), you would respond on hand (1). When instead he opens 1NT, you know that the combined point-count is 22-24 points and you should pass.

Hand (2) is not strong enough for game either, but you would like to make hearts trumps. You do this by responding 2♦, a transfer response. Partner will bid 2♥ and you will then pass.

Perhaps you would like to make diamonds trumps on hand (3). Sorry! The response of 2♦ is a transfer to hearts, so you must pass 1NT. It is no great loss, since the opponents would probably bid one of the majors over a natural 2◊ anyway. Playing transfer responses has many advantages as we will see shortly.

The responder makes a game try

When the responder begins with Stayman or a transfer bid, he will have the opportunity to make a game try at his next turn. Your partner opens 1NT and you hold one of these hands:

(4)	♠ Q 9 7	(5)	♠ K J 9 8 7 4	(6)	♠ K 8 2
	♡ K 10 7 6 4		♡ 8 2		♡ K Q 6 4
	◊ K 8 3		◊ 7 6		◊ J 9 7 2
	♣ J 9		♣ K 6 3		♣ 10 5

On hand (4) you would like to tell partner 'I have five hearts' and 'I want to invite game'. With transfers, you can do exactly that! You begin with 2◊, to show five (or more) hearts. Partner duly rebids 2♡ and you continue with 2NT to invite game. With only 15 points, partner will pass with two hearts and bid 3♡ with three hearts; with four-card support he may decide to bid 4♡. When partner has a reasonable 16 or 17 points, he will bid 4♡ with at least three hearts, otherwise 3NT.

Hand (5) contains only 7 points but is worth more because of the six-card major suit. You respond 2♡ and partner rebids 2♠, as requested. Now you invite a game by advancing to 3♠. Partner will then either pass or raise to 4♠, according to his strength and the quality of his spade support.

On hand (6) you bid 2♣ (Stayman), seeking a 4-4 heart fit. If partner responds 2♡, you will add support points and bid 4♡. If instead he rebids 2◊ (denying a four-card major) or 2♠, you will make a game try of 2NT.

The responder heads for game

When you hear partner open 1NT you will often know immediately that you want to play in a particular game contract. When you have a five-card or longer major suit, you should begin with a transfer so that the 1NT opener can play the contract. This will keep his high cards concealed and prevent an opening lead through his honors. Sometimes you will have to investigate which game will be best.

Partner opens 1NT and you hold one of these hands:

(7)	♠ 8 3	(8)	♠ K 8	(9)	♠ 9
	♡ A J 8 7 2		♡ 7 5		♡ A Q 8 5
	◊ A 10 3		◊ A Q 10 6 4 3		◊ 7 6 4 2
	♣ Q 9 4		♣ 9 8 6		♣ K Q 8 2

You have enough for game on hand (7) and would like to end in 4♡ when partner has heart support, or in 3NT when he does not. You show the hearts with a 2♢ transfer and partner dutifully bids 2♡. Now you bid 3NT, passing the message: 'I have enough for game. Please choose between 3NT and 4♡.' Partner will bid 4♡ when he has three or more hearts, and pass 3NT with only two of them.

There is only one good response on hand (8). You should raise directly to 3NT. A diamond game would require eleven tricks instead of the nine required for 3NT to succeed. 5♢ is almost certainly out of reach when you hold only 9 HCP in the responding hand. Your diamond suit will be a welcome sight to partner in 3NT and may yield six tricks on its own.

On hand (9) you start with 2♣ (Stayman), hoping to find a heart fit. If partner rebids 2♡, you raise to 4♡. If he responds 2♢ or 2♠ instead, you bid 3NT next. There is no point worrying that the spades may be unprotected. Partner is most likely to hold honor cards in the suit where you have none, particularly as you hold only one card there. In any case, 3NT is much more likely to make than 5♣ or 5♢ (even if you happen to have a fit in a minor).

The responder considers a slam

When the responder holds 16 points or more, or a good hand with a particularly strong suit, his thoughts may turn towards a slam. Suppose partner opens 1NT and you hold one of these hands:

(10) ♠ A J 7	(11) ♠ K 4	(12) ♠ 2
♡ K 10	♡ A 10 7	♡ A K J 9 7 6 2
♢ Q 9 7 5	♢ A Q 8 6 3	♢ 8 3
♣ A Q 8 6	♣ K J 3	♣ A Q 4

To bid a slam with hand (10) you need partner to be upper-range within his announced 15-17 HCP. You can issue a slam invitation by bidding a natural 4NT. (A raise of 1NT or 2NT to 4NT is not ace-asking.) Partner will then decide whether to pass or to bid 6NT. If he decides to accept the try and he happens to hold a five-card suit, he may bid six of that suit. If partner were to rebid 6♠, 6♢ or 6♣, for example, you would be happy to pass that.

Hand (11) has 17 HCP and a strong diamond suit. You will raise directly to 6NT.

Hand (12) offers excellent slam potential because the heart suit is a source of tricks. You will start with 3♡. If partner likes the idea of slam, he will cooperate by **cuebidding a control**, an idea we will look at in Chapter 14. If partner does not like his hand for slam, he will sign off in 3NT or 4♡.

Bidding a second suit

We have already seen that the responder can follow a transfer bid with a further bid in his long suit or in notrump. Another option is to show a second suit. Such a rebid is game-forcing. Remember that there is no point in showing a minor suit unless you are strong enough to contemplate playing in an eleven-trick game there. How will you respond to 1NT on these hands?

(13) ♠ 8
     ♡ K Q 8 7 2
     ◇ A K 10 7
     ♣ J 10 4

(14) ♠ K 10 9 7 6
     ♡ 7
     ◇ Q 4 3
     ♣ A 9 8 6

(15) ♠ A 10 9 6 5
     ♡ K J 8 6 2
     ◇ Q 6
     ♣ 5

With two good suits and a full 13 HCP on hand (13), you are strong enough to follow the sequence: 1NT - 2◇; 2♡ - 3◇. Partner can then show heart support, or bid 3NT with stoppers in the black suits. He can also raise diamonds, since you would not have rebid 3◇ unless you were strong enough to contemplate 5◇.

On (14) you show the spades with 2♡, partner responding 2♠. Next you should bid 3NT, asking partner to choose between 3NT and 4♠. You should not rebid 3♣ because you are too weak to think of playing in 5♣. When partner holds only two spades, you want to end in 3NT.

On hand (15) you want to play in either 4♠ or 4♡. You show the higher-ranking suit, spades, first with a transfer bid of 2♡. When partner rebids 2♠, as required, you rebid 4♡. This suggests 5-5 shape in the majors and offers a choice of games. Partner will either pass or bid 4♠.

Similarly you can bid a second suit after making a Stayman enquiry:

(16) ♠ 8
      ♡ A Q J 8
      ◇ 6 4 3
      ♣ A Q 7 6 2

(17) ♠ A K 10 6
      ♡ 5
      ◇ K Q J 9 6
      ♣ 9 6 2

Partner opens 1NT and you bid 2♣ (Stayman) on hand (16), looking for a 4-4 heart fit. If partner responds 2◇ or 2♠, denying four hearts, you can continue 3♣ on the next round. This is forcing to game and shows 5+ cards in clubs. With 13 HCP opposite 15-17, you are entitled to offer clubs as a trump suit. If instead you held only 9 points, you would rebid 3NT, hoping for the best as far as the spade suit was concerned.

On (17) the bidding starts 1NT - 2♣; 2♡. Partner would respond 2♡ when he held four hearts along with four spades, so there may still be a 4-4 spade fit. You continue with a natural and forcing 3◇. When partner does hold four spades, he will bid 3♠ now. You have not raised the hearts and he expects you to hold a four-card major because you used the Stayman convention.

Responding to 1NT — Problems A

1.   ♠ J 10 4   ♡ 9 6   ◇ K 10 9 6 5   ♣ A 8 7

Partner opens 1NT. What action will you take?

      (a) Pass   (b) 2◇   (c) 2NT

2.   ♠ Q 8   ♡ A J 6 5   ◇ 6 3   ♣ K J 7 6 4

Partner opens 1NT. What is your response and what sequence are you planning?

      (a) 2♣   (b) 3♣   (c) 3NT

3.   ♠ 9 2   ♡ J 3   ◇ 6 4 3   ♣ A K 10 8 7 2

Partner opens 1NT. What action will you take?

      (a) Pass   (b) 3♣   (c) 3NT

4.   ♠ A Q 7 6 3   ♡ 6 5   ◇ K 8   ♣ J 10 6 5

Partner opens 1NT. What response will you make? What sequence of bids do you have in mind?

      (a) 2♣   (b) 2♡   (c) 3NT

5.   ♠ 4   ♡ A J 8 7 5 2   ◇ J 8 6 2   ♣ Q 2

Partner opens 1NT. What is your response and what sequence are you planning?

      (a) 2◇   (b) 3♡   (c) 4♡

(The answers are overleaf.)

Responding to 1NT — Solutions A

1.   ♠J 10 4   ♡9 6   ◇K 10 9 6 5   ♣A 8 7

You cannot bid 2◇ because this would be a transfer bid, showing hearts. Although you have only 8 HCP, you have extra values in the two tens and the five-card diamond suit. You are worth a game try of 2NT. **Answer:** (c) 2NT.

2.   ♠Q 8   ♡A J 6 5   ◇6 3   ♣K J 7 6 4

You have enough for game, but not for an eleven-trick game in clubs. You should start with 2♣ (Stayman). If partner responds 2♡, you will raise to 4♡. Otherwise you will bid 3NT. **Answer:** (a) 2♣.

3.   ♠9 2   ♡J 3   ◇6 4 3   ♣A K 10 8 7 2

When you respond to a 1NT or 2NT opening bid and you have a five-card suit headed by the ace or king, add 1 point; if your suit is six cards, add 2 points. You should respond 3NT here, a contract that partner will have a great chance of making. It is a mistake to respond 3♣, thinking: 'I want partner to rebid 3NT'. If you want to be in 3NT, bid it yourself! In any case, a response of 3♣ shows a much stronger hand, one on which you think a slam may be possible. **Answer:** (c) 3NT .

4.   ♠A Q 7 6 3   ♡6 5   ◇K 8   ♣J 10 6 5

With a five-card spade suit, you should respond with a 2♡ transfer bid rather than 2♣ (Stayman). Stayman is used when you are seeking a fit for a four-card major suit. Over partner's 2♠ rebid, you should say 3NT. This will ask partner to choose between 3NT and 4♠. You should not bid your clubs on a hand of this strength, since you have no intention of playing in 5♣. **Answer:** (b) 2♡.

5.   ♠4   ♡A J 8 7 5 2   ◇J 8 6 2   ♣Q 2

You can add a couple of points for your six-card major and this means that you should head for game. It is better to bid 2◇ first, raising partner's 2♡ rebid to 4♡. By allowing partner to play the contract, you will keep his honor cards hidden and prevent a possibly damaging lead though his high cards. **Answer:** (a) 2◇.

Responding to 1NT — Problems B

6.   ♠ K Q 8 7 3 2   ♡ A 6   ◇ K Q 5   ♣ Q 8

Partner opens 1NT. What action will you take?

    (a) 2♡   (b) 3♠   (c) 4♠

7.   ♠ Q 8 4   ♡ A 7 5   ◇ K Q 6 5   ♣ A J 2

You open 1NT and the bidding continues 2◇; 2♡ - 2NT. What sort of hand does partner have? What will you bid next?

    (a) Pass   (b) 3♡   (c) 3NT   (d) 4♡

8.   ♠ A 7   ♡ A J 6   ◇ Q 10 5 2   ♣ A J 9 2

You open 1NT and the bidding continues 2♡; 2♠ - 3♣. What sort of hand does partner have? What will you bid next?

    (a) 3♠   (b) 3NT   (c) 4♣   (d) 5♣

9.   ♠ K J 6 5   ♡ K Q 7 3   ◇ A 8 2   ♣ K 10

You open 1NT and the bidding continues 2♣; 2♡ - 3NT. What will you say now?

    (a) Pass   (b) 4♠

10.   ♠ K 10 2   ♡ A J 7 6   ◇ K 4   ♣ A J 10 5

You open 1NT and the bidding continues 2♣; 2♡ - 3♡. What sort of hand does partner hold? What will you say next?

    (a) Pass   (b) 3NT   (c) 4♡

(The answers are overleaf.)

Responding to 1NT — Solutions B

6.   ♠ K Q 8 7 3 2   ♡ A 6   ◇ K Q 5   ♣ Q 8

Suppose you start with a 2♡ transfer bid, partner rebidding 2♠. What can you say next? Not an easy question to answer! Instead of transferring to spades with 2♡ over 1NT, you need to find a response that tells partner straight away that you have long spades and slam interest. That bid is 3♠. Partner may then show little enthusiasm by bidding 3NT. With a trump fit but not a particularly great hand for a slam, he can bid 4♠. With a useful hand and a fit, he may cuebid an ace or bid 4NT to ask for aces (or keycards), see Chapter 14. **Answer:** (b) 3♠.

7.   ♠ Q 8 4   ♡ A 7 5   ◇ K Q 6 5   ♣ A J 2

You open 1NT and the bidding continues 2◇; 2♡ - 2NT. Partner has five hearts and enough strength to invite a game. You are happy to play in hearts, with your three-card support. Should you bid 3♡ or 4♡? Your hand contains 16 points, in the middle of the range, but you have no tens and depressing 4-3-3-3 shape. You should decline the game try by rebidding 3♡. **Answer:** (b) 3♡.

8.   ♠ A 7   ♡ A J 6   ◇ Q 10 5 2   ♣ A J 9 2

You open 1NT and the bidding continues 2♡; 2♠ - 3♣. Your partner has shown five spades and at least four clubs. What's more, he has shown a hand that is strong enough to contemplate at least an eleven-trick club game. You have wonderful support for clubs: four trumps and three aces. You are very happy to raise to 4♣ and the bidding may well continue to 6♣. **Answer:** (c) 4♣.

9.   ♠ K J 6 5   ♡ K Q 7 3   ◇ A 8 2   ♣ K 10

The bidding starts 1NT - 2♣; 2♡ - 3NT. How easy it would be to pass now, but this would be a mistake! Why did partner use Stayman? He hasn't raised your 2♡ response, so he can't have four hearts. He must hold four spades or he wouldn't have bid 2♣ in the first place. You should now bid 4♠. **Answer:** (b) 4♠.

10.   ♠ K 10 2   ♡ A J 7 6   ◇ K 4   ♣ A J 10 5

The bidding starts 1NT - 2♣; 2♡ - 3♡. Partner holds four hearts and enough strength to invite a game. You have a mid-range 16 points. Should you pass or bid 4♡? Your hand contains two positive features: you have two tens and you have a doubleton diamond, which may allow partner to score a ruffing trick or two. You should gladly accept his invitation, raising to the heart game. **Answer:** (c) 4♡.

Responding to 1NT — Problems C

11. ♠ A J 8 4   ♡ A 6   ◇ K J 5 3   ♣ K 10 8

You open 1NT and the bidding continues 2♣; 2♠ - 3◇. What does partner's bidding mean. What will you say next?

    (a) Pass   (b) 3NT   (c) 4◇

12. ♠ Q 8 4   ♡ A 7 5   ◇ K Q 6 5   ♣ A J 2

You open 1NT and the bidding continues 2♡; 2♠ - 3NT. What sort of hand does partner have? What will you bid next?

    (a) Pass   (b) 4♠   (c) 4NT

13. ♠ K 10 3   ♡ A Q 6   ◇ A J 7 6 2   ♣ Q 9

You open 1NT and partner responds 2NT. What action will you take?

    (a) Pass   (b) 3◇   (c) 3NT

14. ♠ A 7 6   ♡ K 3   ◇ A 9 5   ♣ K J 10 7 2

You open 1NT and the bidding continues 2♡; 2♠ - 4♡. What will you say now?

    (a) Pass   (b) 4♠   (c) 4NT

15. ♠ 10 2   ♡ A K Q 6   ◇ K 8 4 2   ♣ A 10 5

You open 1NT and partner responds 3♣. What will you say next?

    (a) 3◇   (b) 3♡   (c) 4♣

(The answers are overleaf.)

Responding to 1NT — Solutions C

11.   ♠ A J 8 4   ♡ A 6   ♢ K J 5 3   ♣ K 10 8

The bidding starts 1NT - 2♣; 2♠ - 3♢. Your partner's 3♢ continuation is forcing and natural, suggesting five diamonds. He will also hold four hearts to justify the Stayman bid at the start. Your partner would not introduce diamonds (a minor suit) unless he was strong enough to consider an eleven-trick game in that suit. You have four-card support for diamonds, giving you a nine-card fit, and good controls (aces and kings). You have no excuse whatsoever for failing to support partner's diamonds! **Answer:** (c) 4♢.

12.   ♠ Q 8 4   ♡ A 7 5   ♢ K Q 6 5   ♣ A J 2

You open 1NT and the bidding continues 2♡; 2♠ - 3NT. Your partner has five spades and is offering you a choice between 3NT and 4♠. Since you have three-card spade support you should bid 4♠. Do not think that you should give 3NT a try, just because your hand is so flat. Partner might hold a singleton heart, for example. He would not introduce a four-card club suit on 5-1-3-4 shape unless his hand was strong enough to support an eleven-trick game in clubs. **Answer:** (b) 4♠.

13.   ♠ K 10 3   ♡ A Q 6   ♢ A J 7 6 2   ♣ Q 9

You open 1NT and partner bids 2NT. This is a game try. Partner is asking you to decide whether to pass or go to 3NT. Your 16 HCP is in the middle of the 15-17 range. However, your five-card diamond suit, headed by a couple of honors, is worth a bit extra. You should have no hesitation in raising to 3NT. **Answer:** (c) 3NT.

14.   ♠ A 7 6   ♡ K 3   ♢ A 9 5   ♣ K J 10 7 2

You open 1NT and the bidding continues 2♡; 2♠ - 4♡. The 2♡ response shows five spades and the 4♡ rebid shows five hearts. Since you prefer spades to hearts, you should bid 4♠ now. You have no reason to think that partner has anything beyond game values, so there is no case for bidding 4NT. **Answer:** (b) 4♠.

15.   ♠ 10 2   ♡ A K Q 6   ♢ K 8 4 2   ♣ A 10 5

You open 1NT and partner bids 3♣. He has at least six clubs and is suggesting a slam. You have three-card club support and a possible ruffing value in spades. In addition, your high cards are 'prime' — they are aces and kings, not queens and jacks. You should agree clubs as trumps by raising to 4♣. **Answer:** (c) 4♣.

PART II

HIGHER-LEVEL OPENING BIDS

7

PREEMPTIVE OPENINGS AND RESPONSES

There are two main objectives behind the bids that you make. The first is for you and your partner to describe your hands so that you can judge what your best contract will be. The other is to take away bidding space from the opponents so they will find it difficult to determine their own best contract. In this chapter we will look at opening weak two- and three-bids, which are obstructive in nature. Their aim is to prevent the opposing side from bidding accurately.

The weak two opening bid

Opening bids of 2◊, 2♡ and 2♠ show 6-10 HCP and a six-card suit. (As we will see in Chapter 8, 2♣ is a special opening bid reserved for very strong hands.) In the early days of a bridge career it is best to take a disciplined approach to such openings. You should use them when you have a fairly impressive suit. Typically it will contain two of the three top honors or three of the top five honors. Look at these hands:

(1)	♠ A Q 10 8 6 3	(2)	♠ 10 7 3	(3)	♠ 5
	♡ J 6		♡ Q J 8 7 6 3		♡ J 10 9 2
	◊ 10 9 5		◊ 9 2		◊ A K J 7 6 2
	♣ 8 3		♣ A 4		♣ 10 5 2

Hand (1) is a standard down-the-middle weak 2♠. You have a respectable six-card suit and 7 points. Your opponents are likely to have more points than your side. Just imagine how much harder it will be for them to discover their best contract when you remove nearly two whole levels of bidding!

What about hand (2)? We have to admit that many players would open 2♡ on this hand and it's not a mistake to do so. If you haven't played weak two-bids before, however, you may feel more comfortable waiting until you hold a better suit.

Hand (3) contains a fine six-card diamond suit, easily good enough for a 2◊ opening. Again, you will find players who would open 2◊ on that hand. But it's a bit risky in the first two seats because you might miss a heart game if partner has reasonable values and length in hearts. In general, you should avoid opening a weak two when you have a four-card major on the side unless partner is a passed hand.

You get the picture, then. You can either play disciplined weak twos or open them more often, on a wider range of hands. By following the latter approach, you will cause more problems for the opponents. You may also cause quite a few for your partner!

Responding to weak two-bids

These are the main responses to an opening bid of 2♡:

2♠/3♣/3◊	forcing
2NT	game try, asks opener to bid a side-suit ace or king
3♡	preemptive
4♡	may be strong or preemptive
3NT/4♠	to play

How good a hand do you need to make game in partner's suit opposite a weak two-bid? It is not merely a question of points. Because partner is likely to be fairly short in all the side suits, aces and kings may be worth very much more than queens and jacks. Look at this pair of hands:

WEST	EAST	WEST	EAST
♠ A Q 8 7 4 2	♠ J 6	2♠	4♠
♡ 9 6	♡ A K 8 3		
◊ Q 10 4	◊ J 9 6		
♣ 5 2	♣ A Q 9 7		

The spade game is a reasonable contract. You have two certain diamond losers and one trump loser. To make the game it is likely that you will need the club finesse to succeed. You will also need the trumps to break reasonably, to avoid two losers in that suit. It's worth bidding 4♠ but only just. When instead you have 12 or 13 points and a balanced hand, it will often be right to pass 2♠. So, remember that you need quite a good hand to raise a weak two-bid to game. When you have a singleton in partner's long suit, you need a very good hand to head for game. Many players overbid when responding to a weak two-bid.

Let's say that your partner opens 2♡ and you hold one of these hands:

(4) ♠ A Q 9 7	(5) ♠ Q 7 4	(6) ♠ 8 4 2
♡ 6	♡ A 10 8 2	♡ K Q 6 4
◊ A K 8 3	◊ K Q J 4	◊ K 10 9 8 5
♣ Q 7 6 2	♣ A 3	♣ 5

On hand (4), with no heart support, you should pass. Suppose partner's trump holding is: ♡AQ9762. In a heart contract, he might easily lose three trumps and two clubs, maybe a spade too. Playing in notrump would be even worse, since you would probably score only one or two heart tricks. Remember that there are likely no entries to partner's weak hand.

With hand (5) you would raise to 4♡, expecting to score six hearts, two diamonds, the ♣A and another trick from somewhere. On hand (6) you don't expect to make 4♡ but you should raise to 4♡ nevertheless. By removing even more bidding space, you hope to make life difficult for the opponents. They can probably make a good contract in spades or clubs.

The weak three opening bid

An opening bid at the three-level shows a weak hand with a suit of seven cards or more. By removing so much bidding space from your opponents, you make it extremely difficult for them to bid their hands accurately. You should be fairly bold with such openings. Don't worry unduly that you may be doubled and go for a big penalty. For one thing, most pairs play takeout doubles of weak three-bids (also of weak two-bids). Instead, your thoughts should be: 'They will have a very easy time if I don't open 3♡ here.'

As a general rule, you should have reasonably good playing strength (a good suit) when you open a three-bid in the first two seats. Your partner may have a strong hand and you don't want to take away bidding space from your own side. You should also be conservative when you are vulnerable, since the potential penalties are more if the opponents do manage to double you. When instead you are in the third position and the first two players have passed, you can afford to be bolder with your three-bids. Be willing to open on a fairly weak suit. Remember that if the bidding starts 3◇ - (dbl), this will nearly always be for takeout.

Look at these potential preemptive three-bids:

(7)	♠ 9	(8)	♠ A 10 8 7 6 3 2	(9)	♠ Q 10 9 7 6 5 3
	♡ 10 3		♡ 8		♡ 8 5 2
	◇ K Q J 9 8 6 2		◇ A 10 7		◇ K 5
	♣ J 9 4		♣ J 3		♣ 8

Hand (7) contains a splendid seven-card suit. You would open 3◇ in any seat and at any vulnerability. Those who say to themselves 'I like a little bit more when vulnerable' will never go very far in the game. You must look on the positive side, visualizing just how much more difficult it will be for the opponents to bid their hands when they have to enter the auction at the three-level instead of the one-level.

Hand (8) is not suitable for a preempt. The spades have no solidity and your two aces will give you good defense against any contract played by the other side. A sound guideline that a hand is suitable for preemption is that it will make a lot of tricks if you get to choose trumps and very few if the opponents choose trumps.

Hand (9) is the sort of hand on which you would open 3♠ when not vulnerable and sitting in the third seat. You can be fairly confident that the player on your left holds a good hand. Remember that if he doubles, this will be for takeout.

How about responding to a weak three-bid? Imagine that partner has opened, say, 3♠. There are two possible reasons to raise to 4♠. The first is that you hold enough aces and kings, or trump support, to expect the game to be made. The second is that you have good trump support and want to raise preemptively to make the opponents' task even more difficult. Since they do not know which type of raise you have, you may even avoid a double. When you raise preemptively and are doubled, you expect the resultant penalty to be less than the opponents could have made when playing in their own best contract.

Two important things to remember about opening preempts

1) If your hand totals 13 or more points with distribution, open with one of a suit: do not preempt.
2) Do not preempt if the bidding has gone pass-pass-pass to you. We never preempt in the passout seat — better to have no score than a minus score.

Preemptive openings — Problems A

1.   ♠ 8 4 ♡ A K 9 6 ◇ A 10 9 ♣ A J 10 4

Your partner opens 2♠. What action will you take?

     (a) 2NT (game try)   (b) 3NT   (c) 4♠

2.   ♠ 9 8 2 ♡ K Q 10 9 5 2 ◇ 3 ♣ K 10 6

You open 2♡ and partner responds 2NT, asking for a feature. What action will you take?

     (a) 3♣   (b) 3♡   (c) 4♡

3.   ♠ K J 6 ♡ 8 7 5 ◇ 10 2 ♣ K Q 8 7 4

Partner opens 2♠. What will you say now?

     (a) Pass   (b) 3♣   (c) 3♠

4.   ♠ A Q 10 9 7 3 ♡ 6 ◇ A J 9 ♣ A 10 4

Partner opens 2♡. What response will you make?

     (a) Pass   (b) 2♠   (c) 3♠

5.   ♠ K 9 7 5 4 2 ♡ 8 3 ◇ 6 2 ♣ K 10 8

Under what conditions would you open 2♠?

     (a) Never   (b) Not vulnerable   (c) Not vulnerable in third seat

(The answers are overleaf.)

Preemptive openings — Solutions A

1.　　　　　♠ 8 4　♡ A K 9 6　◇ A 10 9　♣ A J 10 4

Your partner opens 2♠. You are just about worth a raise to 4♠. If his trumps are ♠KQJ962, you will probably have five trump tricks and four top winners. If he holds two or three low clubs in addition, you may be able to take two club finesses for an extra trick. If instead his trumps are ♠AQJ875, you may be able to score six trump tricks with a repeated finesse. A contract of 3NT would often be hopeless; you could be cut off from dummy's spade suit. **Answer:** (c) 4♠.

2.　　　　　♠ 9 8 2　♡ K Q 10 9 5 2　◇ 3　♣ K 10 6

You open 2♡ and partner bids 2NT, asking for a feature. You have the ♣K, so you show it. Partner might have a hand like ♠53 ♡J43 ◇AQ7 ♣AQJ32, in which case he will be delighted to hear you have the ♣K. **Answer:** (a) 3♣.

3.　　　　　♠ K J 6　♡ 8 7 5　◇ 10 2　♣ K Q 8 7 4

Partner opens 2♠ and you do not expect to make 4♠. Indeed, if partner holds ♠AQ10742 and nothing much else, you may score only 7 or 8 tricks. Since you have little defense to a red-suit contract, you should raise preemptively to 3♠. This is not a game try; you would respond 2NT if you had genuine game interest. **Answer:** (c) 3♠.

4.　　　　　♠ A Q 10 9 7 3　♡ 6　◇ A J 9　♣ A 10 4

Partner opens 2♡. If he holds, say, ♡KQJ962 and little else, you will lose a lot of tricks in a spade contract. If instead partner holds a good weak two including two or three spades, the ♡A and a minor-suit king, you may make 4♠. You should test the waters by responding 2♠, which is forcing for one round. **Answer:** (b) 2♠.

5.　　　　　♠ K 9 7 5 4 2　♡ 8 3　◇ 6 2　♣ K 10 8

The first two players pass. In the third seat it is often worth bidding on hands that you would normally not open. After two passes, you can visualize that your LHO has a strong hand. So, open 2♠ when non-vulnerable and in the third seat. You will often see players opening 2♠ on this type of hand in other situations. It may work, it may not. It is much more of a gamble. **Answer:** (c) 2♠ not vulnerable in third seat.

Preemptive openings — Problems B

6.   ♠ 3   ♡ A J   ◇ A K Q J 5 3 2   ♣ K 10 7

Partner opens 3♠. What action will you take?

     (a) 3NT   (b) 4◇   (c) 4♠

7.   ♠ A J 4   ♡ 5   ◇ Q 10 8 7 6 4   ♣ J 9 2

Partner opens 3♠. What action will you take as responder? Does it depend on the vulnerability?

     (a) Pass   (b) 4♠

8.   ♠ 7   ♡ Q 10 6 4   ◇ A K 10 7 6 3 2   ♣ J

What action will you take, sitting in the first seat with neither side vulnerable?

     (a) Pass   (b) 1◇   (c) 3◇

9.   ♠ A K 6   ♡ 3   ◇ A Q 7 4 2   ♣ K Q 5 4

Partner opens 3♡. What will you say now?

     (a) Pass   (b) 3NT   (c) 4♡

10.   ♠ K Q J 10 6 3 2   ♡ A K 3   ◇ 6 4   ♣ A

Partner opens 3◇. What will you respond?

     (a) 3♠   (b) 4♠   (c) 5◇

(The answers are overleaf.)

Preemptive openings — Solutions B

6.   ♠3 ♡A J ◇A K Q J 5 3 2 ♣K 10 7

Partner opens 3♠. Your best chance of making a game is to respond 3NT. Partner is not allowed to go back to 4♠. He has already described the nature of his hand and must trust that you know what you're doing. **Answer:** (a) 3NT.

7.   ♠A J 4 ♡5 ◇Q 10 8 7 6 4 ♣J 9 2

Partner opens 3♠. You expect that the opponents can make 4♡, maybe 6♡. At any vulnerability you should raise to 4♠. You expect to score seven trump tricks, plus one or two ruffs in the heart suit. Do not dwell solely on the risk that you might go 500 down against a non-vulnerable game. Think instead how incredibly difficult it will be for the opponents to judge their subsequent bidding. **Answer:** (b) 4♠.

8.   ♠7 ♡Q 10 6 4 ◇A K 10 7 6 3 2 ♣J

You are much too strong for a preemptive 3◇, even when vulnerable. If partner held as little as ♡AK732 and a black-suit ace, he would pass 3◇ when you could make twelve tricks in hearts! Although you hold only 10 HCP, you are entitled to add extra points for your splendid seven-card suit and the good shape outside. You should open 1◇. If opening a one-bid on so few points does not appeal to you, then it is better to pass than open 3◇. **Answer:** (b) 1◇.

9.   ♠A K 6 ♡3 ◇A Q 7 4 2 ♣K Q 5 4

Partner opens 3♡ and you have to calculate the best final contract. The first point to note is that 3NT is likely to be hopeless. Partner's heart suit would not contribute at all as his hand will usually contain no entries. A much better chance is that you can make 4♡, by adding partner's trump tricks to the top cards in your hand. Suppose partner has ♡KQJxxxx and little else. You should be able to score six trump tricks plus at least four side-suit winners in your hand. **Answer:** (c) 4♡.

10.   ♠K Q J 10 6 3 2 ♡A K 3 ◇6 4 ♣A

Partner opens 3◇. If he has a good diamond suit, you might be able to make 5◇. However, you can see your own wonderful spades and you must have an excellent chance of making 4♠. Six spade tricks, plus your three side-suit winners give you a total of nine tricks. You have every chance of a diamond trick too. A response of 3♠ would be forcing but since you do not need spade support, you should go straight to the spade game. **Answer:** (b) 4♠.

Preemptive openings — Problems C

11.   ♠ K 8 ♡ A Q 10 7 6 3 ◇ 10 9 4 ♣ 6 2

You open 2♡ and partner responds 2♠. What action will you take?

    (a) Pass   (b) 3♡   (c) 3♠

12.   ♠ A J 10 7 6 2 ♡ K 10 4 ◇ 10 5 ♣ 9 8

You open 2♠ and hear a 3◇ response. What action will you take?

    (a) Pass   (b) 3♡   (c) 3♠   (d) 3NT

13.   ♠ K 10 8 7 5 4 2 ♡ 9 3 ◇ Q 8 7 ♣ J

Partner and your RHO pass. What action will you take and does your vulnerability affect the decision?

    (a) Pass   (b) 2♠   (c) 3♠

14.   ♠ A K J 7 ♡ 3 ◇ A Q 7 2 ♣ A K 6 4

Partner opens 3♡. What response will you make?

    (a) 3NT   (b) 4♡   (c) 4NT

15.   ♠ 10 8 2 ♡ J 3 ◇ K Q J 7 6 2 ♣ 9 4

You are not vulnerable and the first two players pass. What will you bid?

    (a) Pass   (b) 2◇   (c) 3◇

(The answers are overleaf.)

Preemptive openings — Solutions C

11.   ♠K 8 ♡A Q 10 7 6 3 ◇10 9 4 ♣6 2

You open 2♡ and partner bids 2♠. A change of suit is *forcing for one round*. If your partner sees the chance of game in spades, he will hold a good hand almost certainly with six spades. Rebidding 3♡ would not be a good idea. Your partner already knows that you have six hearts. Instead you should raise to 3♠. Knowing that you can assist him in the spade suit will often allow him to bid a good spade game. **Answer:** (c) 3♠.

12.   ♠A J 10 7 6 2 ♡K 10 4 ◇10 5 ♣9 8

You open 2♠ and partner bids 3◇. You have to bid again, whatever you hold. Tell partner something useful! Bid 3♡ to show a feature (stopper) in hearts. This may be enough to trigger a 3NT bid from your partner. **Answer:** (b) 3♡.

13.   ♠K 10 8 7 5 4 2 ♡9 3 ◇Q 8 7 ♣J

Not vulnerable you should open 3♠ in third seat. The next player is marked with a good hand. If he doubles, this will be for takeout. Vulnerable, and with an unimpressive spade suit, you would not take the risk. There is a small chance that a takeout double by LHO might be left in by your RHO if he has no great shape and a few high cards. You would open just 2♠. **Answer** vul: (b) 2♠, not vul: (c) 3♠.

14.   ♠A K J 7 ♡3 ◇A Q 7 2 ♣A K 6 4

Partner opens 3♡. It is too ambitious to think of a slam. Even if your side is vulnerable, you cannot expect partner to hold ♡AKQxxxx. With such a suit many players would open 4♡. Suppose instead that you are facing ♡KQJxxxx. With no side entry to dummy, to reach any established cards in hearts, a contract of 3NT will be hopeless! You should raise to 4♡, adding your high cards to partner's trump tricks. **Answer:** (b) 4♡.

15.   ♠10 8 2 ♡J 3 ◇K Q J 7 6 2 ♣9 4

The first two players pass and you are not vulnerable. You will hear players say 'Anything goes in the third seat'. Yes, indeed! Here you have virtually no defense against a major-suit game and can expect to make a fair number of tricks in diamonds. You should open 3◇. Don't even think that you are being a bit daring. It is the 'normal opening bid' on such a hand in the third seat. If you were vulnerable, you might well show some caution and open just 2◇. **Answer:** (c) 3◇.

8

2♣ AND 2NT OPENINGS

On most unbalanced hands you will open one of a suit. When you have such a strong unbalanced hand that you think game will be worth bidding even if partner has virtually nothing, you use bridge's strongest opening bid — an artificial 2♣.

With a balanced hand of 20-21 HCP, you open 2NT. On an even stronger balanced hand you open 2♣ and rebid in notrump at the appropriate level. In this chapter we will look at the opening bids of 2♣ and 2NT and at the subsequent bidding.

The 2NT opening

A balanced hand in the 20-21 HCP range is described immediately by opening 2NT. It will then be easy for partner to evaluate how high you should play. These are sound 2NT openings:

(1)		(2)		(3)	
♠	A J 4	♠	K Q J	♠	K Q 10 7 6
♡	Q 6	♡	A 10	♡	A K 2
◇	A Q 9 7	◇	A Q 10 8 3 2	◇	K 7
♣	A K 10 2	♣	A 8	♣	A J 3

Open 2NT on hand (1). Don't worry that you do not have a secure heart stopper. With 20 points you would open 2NT on such a hand even if you held a small doubleton somewhere. The bidding would otherwise become unmanageable after opening one of a suit.

You are happy to open 2NT on hand (2). Your shape is only semi-balanced, but if you open 1◇ it will be hard to catch up later. 2NT is easily best on hand (3) as well; the five-card major is no problem whatsoever. Imagine if you opened just 1♠ and partner responded 2♣ or 2◇. There would be no way to let partner know that you held such a giant hand.

Responding to 2NT

The methods available when responding to 2NT are similar to those when responding to 1NT:

3♣	Stayman, asking for a four-card major
3◇	transfer response, showing at least five hearts
3♡	transfer response, showing at least five spades
3NT	to play

These are typical sequences:

WEST	EAST	WEST	EAST
♠ A Q 8	♠ K 10 2	2NT	3♣
♡ Q 7	♡ A 9 6 2	3◇	3NT
◇ K Q J 5	◇ 10 3		
♣ A Q 9 2	♣ 8 7 5 3		

East uses Stayman to look for a 4-4 heart fit. When West rebids 3◇, denying a four-card major, East signs off in 3NT. East would have done the same if West had rebid 3♠ to show four spades.

WEST	EAST	WEST	EAST
♠ A Q 8 4	♠ J 5 3	2NT	3◇
♡ J 10 3	♡ K Q 7 6 4	3♡	3NT
◇ A 5	◇ 9 7	4♡	
♣ A K Q 2	♣ 8 6 4		

East shows his hearts and then rebids 3NT, offering partner a choice of games. West holds three hearts and therefore chooses 4♡. As you see, 3NT would have been at risk after a diamond lead.

WEST	EAST	WEST	EAST
♠ A 7	♠ K J 8 7 5 2	2NT	3♡
♡ A Q 8 5	♡ 9 3	3♠	4♠
◇ K Q 10 4	◇ 7 5 2		
♣ A J 8 2	♣ 10 4		

East has enough for a spade game. He uses a transfer response so that his partner can play the contract and avoid an opening lead through West's honors in the side suits.

WEST	EAST	WEST	EAST
♠ A J 6	♠ K 9 7 3	2NT	4NT
♡ K 10 2	♡ A Q 9	6NT	
◇ A J	◇ K 10 5		
♣ A Q J 7 2	♣ 10 9 4		

East wants to invite a slam in notrump. He responds with a non-forcing 4NT to pass this message (just as a raise of 1NT to 4NT would have done). Although West holds only 20 points, he quite rightly adds a point or two for his excellent five-card club suit. As you see, 6NT is an excellent slam.

The strong 2♣ opening

When you open 2♣ on an unbalanced hand, intending to rebid in a suit, you are committing your side to a game contract at least. Consequently you require a very strong hand. Which of the following powerful hands are worth a 2♣ opening?

(4)	♠ K Q J 10 8 6	(5)	♠ K 7	(6)	♠ 6
	♡ A 6		♡ K Q 8		♡ A K Q J 9
	◇ A K Q		◇ A K Q 10 8 3 2		◇ A K 10 6 5
	♣ A 5		♣ A		♣ K 6

On hand (4) you are virtually certain to make 4♠, even if partner's hand provides no help at all. You open 2♣, planning to rebid 2♠. The auction is then forcing to game.

Similarly you open 2♣ on hand (5). You cannot exactly guarantee a game but your chances of making 3NT will be excellent, even if partner has very little for you. If partner holds a major-suit ace, you will be close to making a slam. Perhaps you think that an opening bid of 1◇ is unlikely to be passed out. That's true, but even if partner does respond you will have a difficult time describing the power of your hand.

On hand (6) a minor-suit queen may be enough to let you make a game contract and you would be nervous of opening just 1♡. After opening 2♣, you will also find it easier to reach a slam if partner has a reasonable hand and a fit for one of your suits.

Opening 2♣ on a balanced hand

We have already seen that you open 2NT with a balanced hand of 20-21 HCP. With stronger balanced hands, you open 2♣, Partner will respond 2◊ unless he has a good suit to show and you rebid according to this scale*:

2♣ - 2◊; 2NT	22-23 HCP
2♣ - 2◊; 3NT	24-25 HCP
Open 3NT	26-27 HCP
2♣ - 2◊; 4NT	28-30 HCP

When you rebid 2NT the subsequent bidding by responder is along the same lines as opposite a 2NT opening:

WEST	EAST	WEST	EAST
♠ A 3	♠ K 10 8 6 4	2♣	2◊
♡ K J 6	♡ 7 5 4	2NT	3♡
◊ A K 10 5	◊ J 2	3♠	3NT
♣ A K J 6	♣ 10 3 2		

East shows his five spades with a 3♡ transfer response and then offers a choice of games. West leaves it in 3NT since he holds only two-card spade support.

WEST	EAST	WEST	EAST
♠ A Q 4	♠ K 10 8	2♣	2◊
♡ A K 10 5	♡ Q 6	3NT	6NT
◊ A 8 3	◊ K 9 7 5		
♣ A K 6	♣ Q 7 4 2		

East holds 10 HCP opposite West's 24-25 HCP and raises directly to 6NT. The slam is a good one. There are eleven tricks on top and several opportunities for a twelfth trick.

---

* These ranges are 'standard', but it is perfectly fine to change them as long as you and your partner are in agreement.

Responding to 2♣

Unless the responder has a good suit to show, he will usually respond with the artificial 'waiting' bid of 2◊. This will allow maximum space for the opener to describe his hand further.

WEST	EAST	WEST	EAST
♠ A Q J 10 3	♠ K 8 2	2♣	2◊
♡ Q 7	♡ K 9 6 2	2♠	3♠
◊ A K Q 5	◊ 10 3	4♠	
♣ A J	♣ 8 7 5 3		

East marks time with a waiting 2◊ response and the opener shows a spade suit. East, with two kings in his hand, is interested in a slam now. He makes the positive move of raising to 3♠. (It would be weaker to bid 4♠, since the bidding is forced to game anyway). West has a fairly minimum hand for his bidding so far, so he signs off in 4♠. East lets the bidding die and they stay at a safe level. A slam would be a very poor contract, as you can see.

WEST	EAST	WEST	EAST
♠ A K 10	♠ Q 8 2	2♣	2◊
♡ Q 7	♡ K 10 8 6 3	3♣	3♡
◊ A 6	◊ K 10	3NT	4♣
♣ A K Q 10 6 5	♣ 9 7 3	6♣	

West shows clubs and East shows hearts. When West signs off in 3NT, East admits to some club support. West is then happy to advance to 6♣. As you see, the contract will be easily made by establishing a heart trick.

WEST	EAST	WEST	EAST
♠ K 9 2	♠ A Q J 10 4	2♣	2♠
♡ K Q	♡ 6 5	3♠	4♠
◊ A K Q J 6	◊ 8 4 2	4NT	5◊
♣ A 5 4	♣ 10 9 6	6♠	

Here East has a good spade suit. If he does not give a positive response of 2♠, he will have difficulty in showing that he has a good suit later. He duly responds 2♠ and West rebids 3♠, setting the suit as trumps. With a minimum positive response, East bids only 4♠ next. West can visualize a slam, facing a positive response. He asks for aces, by bidding a Blackwood 4NT, and bids 6♠ when he hears confirmation that partner holds one ace. Declarer will lose only the ♡A.

Since you will make the same response of 2◊ on hands that contain a few useful cards, as well as on near-busts, it is useful to have a way of telling partner on the second round that you are very weak. When the opener rebids 2♡ or 2♠, a rebid of 3♣ by responder is used for this purpose. This is called a **second negative**.

WEST	EAST	WEST	EAST
♠ A K Q J 8 2	♠ 7 3	2♣	2◇
♡ A Q 5	♡ 9 4 3	2♠	3♣
◇ A	◇ J 8 6 2	3♠	4♠
♣ A K J	♣ 10 7 5 2		

West has a splendid hand. When he first picks it up, he is almost certain that he will reach a slam. East responds 2◇ and then gives a second negative of 3♣ to warn partner that he is very weak. East bids 4♠ at his third turn and West realizes that he has no reason to expect East to help him with the three potential losers in his side suits. He makes a disciplined pass and is pleased that he did so when the dummy appears!

Any other rebid will suggest a useful card or two.

WEST	EAST	WEST	EAST
♠ A K Q J 6	♠ 8 2	2♣	2◇
♡ A K J 8	♡ 10 3	2♠	3◇
◇ A K 4	◇ Q J 8 7 5	3♡	3♠
♣ 8	♣ K 7 5 3	4NT	5♣
		6♠	

East would have given a second negative of 3♣ if he held a poorer hand and no ♣K. Expecting that East's diamonds will allow him to dispose of the ♡J and ♡8, West bids the small slam via a Blackwood 4NT bid, asking for aces.

2♣ and 2NT openings — Problems A

1.   ♠ A Q 6 ♡ K Q 10 ◇ A J 5 ♣ A Q 9 4

What opening bid will you make?

    (a) 1♣   (b) 2♣   (c) 2NT

2.   ♠ 10 7 4 ♡ A Q 7 2 ◇ 9 8 5 ♣ A J 4

Your partner opens 2♣. What will you respond? What is your subsequent bidding plan?

    (a) 2◇   (b) 2♡   (c) 2NT   (d) 3NT

3.   ♠ A 6 ♡ Q 8 7 5 ◇ 9 8 4 ♣ K 10 6 2

The bidding starts 2NT - 3♣; 3♡. What will you say now?

    (a) 3NT   (b) 4♡   (c) 4NT   (d) 6♡

4.   ♠ K 3 ♡ K Q J 8 6 ◇ 10 7 6 4 ♣ 9 2

Partner opens 2♣. What response will you make?

    (a) 2◇   (b) 2♡   (c) 3♡

5.   ♠ A K Q 9 7 6 ♡ 3 ◇ A K Q 2 ♣ K Q

The bidding starts 2♣ - 2◇; 2♠ - 3♠. What will you say now?

    (a) 4◇   (b) 4♠   (c) 4NT

(The answers are overleaf.)

2♣ and 2NT openings — Solutions A

1.   ♠ A Q 6 ♡ K Q 10 ◊ A J 5 ♣ A Q 9 4

In North America a 2NT opening would show 20-21 HCP. Since you have 22 HCP here, you must open 2♣ instead, intending to rebid 2NT. (In Europe it is common for 2NT to show 20-22 HCP, in which case you would open 2NT.) **Answer:** (b) 2♣.

2.   ♠ 10 7 4 ♡ A Q 7 2 ◊ 9 8 5 ♣ A J 4

With 11 HCP including two precious aces, you will be heading into the slam zone. For the moment, you should make the waiting response of 2◊ to see which type of hand the opener has. If he rebids 2NT, showing 22-24 points, you will raise to 6NT. If instead he rebids in a suit, you will agree that suit as trumps with a raise. **Answer:** (a) 2◊.

3.   ♠ A 6 ♡ Q 8 7 5 ◊ 9 8 4 ♣ K 10 6 2

The bidding starts 2NT - 3♣; 3♡. By using Stayman, you have found a 4-4 heart fit. The question is: do you have enough for a slam? Partner has shown 20-21 HCP, so it would be too ambitious to invite a slam. You should raise to 4♡. **Answer:** (b) 4♡.

4.   ♠ K 3 ♡ K Q J 8 6 ◊ 10 7 6 4 ♣ 9 2

Partner opens 2♣. You should respond 2♡ to show a useful suit of (at least) five cards. Suppose instead you were to make the waiting response of 2◊ and partner then rebid 3♣. You would bid 3♡ next but partner would have little idea whether you had a good suit or just any old five-card suit. **Answer:** (b) 2♡.

5.   ♠ A K Q 9 7 6 ♡ 3 ◊ A K Q 2 ♣ K Q

The bidding starts 2♣ - 2◊; 2♠ - 3♠. Partner's single raise is a strong move that shows a spade fit and at least an ace or a king somewhere. You should bid 4NT to ask for aces. You will sign off in 5♠ if he has no ace, advance to 6♠ if he has one ace and to 7♠ if he has two aces. (With no ace or king, your partner would rebid 4♠ instead of 3♠ and you would pass. Remember that your 2♠ bid was game-forcing, however weak the responder is.) **Answer:** (c) 4NT.

2♣ and 2NT openings — Problems B

6.   ♠A 7 ♡A Q 9 7 6 ♢A K 4 ♣K J 5

You open 2NT and partner responds 4NT. What action will you take?

    (a) Pass   (b) 5♣   (c) 6♡   (d) 6NT

7.   ♠K 4 ♡9 3 ♢K 9 8 5 3 2 ♣10 7 6

The bidding starts 2♣ - 2♢; 2NT. What action will you take as responder?

    (a) 3♢   (b) 3NT   (c) 5♢   (d) 6♢

8.   ♠K Q 7 ♡A K 8 ♢A K J 7 6 ♣10 3

What opening bid will you make?

    (a) 1♢   (b) 2♣   (c) 2NT

9.   ♠9 6 ♡A J 6 5 ♢K Q 10 4 2 ♣Q 8

The bidding starts 2NT - 3♣; 3♠. What will you bid now?

    (a) 3NT   (b) 4♢   (c) 4NT   (d) 6NT

10.   ♠A J 7 3 2 ♡3 ♢J 4 2 ♣8 7 4 3

The bidding starts 2♣ - 2♢; 3♢ - 3♠; 3NT. What will you say next?

    (a) Pass   (b) 4♢   (c) 4♠   (d) 4NT

(The answers are overleaf.)

2♣ and 2NT openings — Solutions B

6.   ♠ A 7 ♡ A Q 9 7 6 ◇ A K 4 ♣ K J 5

You open 2NT and partner responds 4NT. He is inviting you to go to 6NT if you have an upper-range opening. Not only do you hold 21 HCP instead of 20, you also have a five-card suit. You intend to accept his slam try, but nothing is lost by bidding 6♡ instead of 6NT. This tells partner that you have five hearts, just in case he has heart support and would prefer 6♡ to 6NT. **Answer:** (c) 6♡.

7.   ♠ K 4 ♡ 9 3 ◇ K 9 8 5 3 2 ♣ 10 7 6

Partner opens 2♣. Your suit is not good enough for a positive response of 3◇. You make the waiting response of 2◇ and partner rebids 2NT, showing 22-23 points. It is barely possible to envisage a diamond slam if partner has perfect cards — but they never do! Take the conservative approach and bid 3NT, choosing the nine-trick game. **Answer:** (b) 3NT.

8.   ♠ K Q 7 ♡ A K 8 ◇ A K J 7 6 ♣ 10 3

You are well short of the power to open 2♣. The best opening is 2NT, despite the fact that you have no stopper in clubs. If partner raises to 3NT, the most likely location for his honors is in clubs, where you have nothing. The problem in opening 1◇ instead is not so much that you might miss a game. It's that your hand would be difficult to describe if partner did find a response. **Answer:** (c) 2NT.

9.   ♠ 9 6 ♡ A J 6 5 ◇ K Q 10 4 2 ♣ Q 8

Partner opens 2NT and you bid 3♣ (Stayman) to look for a heart fit. Partner's 3♠ response shows four (or five) spades but denies four hearts. With this shape and 32-33 HCP between the hands, you are entitled to continue towards a slam. The best slam may well be 6◇ if partner has a fit for that suit. You should therefore bid 4◇ next. **Answer:** (b) 4◇.

10.   ♠ A J 7 3 2 ♡ 3 ◇ J 4 2 ♣ 8 7 4 3

The bidding starts 2♣ - 2◇; 3◇. Your spades are worth showing now and you continue with 3♠ in case there is a fit there. The opener signs off in 3NT. You should not pass, though, because you have a useful hand in support of diamonds. Not only do you have a wonderful ace, you have three-card support for partner's diamonds and a singleton heart. You should continue with 4◇. Partner may then be able to ask for aces. **Answer:** (b) 4◇.

PART III

COMPETITIVE BIDDING

9

OVERCALLS AND RESPONSES

An opponent opens and you have enough to enter the auction. There are two main options: an overcall and a takeout double. When you have a good suit, you can simply bid it. When you have reasonable support for all the suits that the opponents haven't bid, you can instead make a takeout double. This asks partner to choose a trump suit (or bid notrump).

We will look at takeout doubles in the next chapter, but you will see that you promise at least an opening bid. For the moment, we turn our attention to overcalls. A one-level overcall, such as 1♠ over 1♣, covers the very wide range of around 7-17 HCP. A non-jump overcall at the two-level, such as 2◊ over 1♡, needs to be stronger and will show more like 12-17 HCP. If you are any stronger you should begin with a takeout double.

A simple overcall in a suit

Your RHO opens 1◊ and you overcall 1♠. What are your possible reasons?

- You want to suggest a good opening lead to partner
- You want to deprive the opponents of bidding space
- You want to contest the partscore
- You may be able to bid a game, or make a profitable sacrifice.

You would overcall 1♠ over 1◊ on each of these hands:

(1)	♠ K Q J 9 4	(2)	♠ A K J 7 6	(3)	♠ J 9 7 6 3 2
	♡ K 7		♡ 10 4 2		♡ A K 6
	◊ 10 3		◊ K 4		◊ A J 4
	♣ 10 9 6 5		♣ A J 8		♣ 5

Hand (1) would not be worth an opening bid but it is worth a one-level overcall. You are bidding a suit that may represent a good opening lead for partner, if the opponents win the auction. If partner can raise your spades, you will be able to contest the auction effectively, perhaps even reaching game if partner is strong. You also deprive the next player of some bidding space, preventing a 1♡ response.

Hand (2) is close to maximum for an overcall of 1♠. If partner raises spades, you will consider bidding 4♠. Hand (3) does not suggest a good opening lead to partner, but with so many points and a six-card major you are keen to enter the bidding. Again, you might make a game if partner raises.

A takeout double would be unsuitable on all three hands because you have no wish to ask partner to choose trumps. Instead you want to suggest to him that spades will be your side's best trump suit.

When you overcall in the fourth seat, after a start such as 1♡ - pass - pass, this is called a **balancing overcall**. You expect partner to hold some points because RHO could not respond to the opening bid. You are therefore entitled to overcall on a hand with up to 3 points fewer than would be required in the second seat.

The 1NT overcall

When your RHO opens one of a suit, a 1NT overcall shows a sound stopper in his suit and about 15-18 HCP (a fraction stronger than a 1NT opening).

(4) ♠ A Q 8 4 (5) ♠ K Q 9
   ♡ K 10 7 2   ♡ Q 9 4
   ◇ K Q 2   ◇ A 9 5 3
   ♣ K 7   ♣ Q 10 2

On hand (4) you would happily overcall 1NT if your RHO opened 1◇, 1♡ or 1♠. If instead he opened 1♣, you would prefer a takeout double, since your club stopper is not great and you have support for the three other suits (see next chapter).

Responding to a 1NT overcall is an easy matter: you use the same methods as when partner has opened 1NT. A 2♣ response is Stayman, 2◇/2♡ are transfers.

Look at hand (5). If RHO opens one of a suit, you are not strong enough for a 1NT overcall; neither is your shape suitable for a double. However, if LHO opened one of a suit and this was followed by two passes, you would be strong enough for a balancing 1NT overcall in the passout seat. This suggests 12-14 points.

Weak jump overcalls

What does it mean when your overcall skips a level, for example 2♡ over your RHO's 1♣? Most players nowadays treat such an overcall as weak, usually with a six-card suit. The emphasis is on removing the opponents' bidding space — the same as when you make a preemptive opening bid.

Suppose your RHO opens 1♣ and you hold one of these hands:

(6)   ♠ K Q J 9 4 2   (7)   ♠ 9 6   (8)   ♠ A 6 4
      ♡ 7 3   ♡ A Q 10 8 5 2   ♡ 10 9 3
      ◇ 10 7   ◇ K 9 3   ◇ A K J 9 8 2
      ♣ Q 6 5   ♣ 4 2   ♣ 5

On hand (6) you bid 2♠. As you see, you are showing a hand similar to a weak 2♠ opening. The question of how disciplined you should be with such overcalls is up to you (as it is with weak two-bids). If you only make such bids with a fairly strong suit, you will protect yourself against a large adverse penalty. However, you will not be able to interfere with the opponents' bidding so often.

    With hand (7) you would venture 2♡ over an opening bid of 1♣ or 1◇. If instead the opening bid was 1♠ it would be too much to jump to 3♡ (particularly when vulnerable). Hand (8) is too strong for a weak jump overcall. You would bid diamonds at the minimum level.

Responding to an overcall

One of the reasons to overcall is to take away bidding space from your opponents. With this aim in mind, you should be keen to raise partner's overcall when you have a trump fit. This may take away even more bidding space. Suppose the bidding starts:

LHO	Partner	RHO	You
1◇	1♠	Pass	?

What action should you take on these hands?

(9)   ♠ K 6 3   (10)   ♠ A 10 5   (11)   ♠ K 10 6 4
      ♡ J 7 2   ♡ K Q 9 4   ♡ 3
      ◇ 10 7 6 2   ◇ 9 3   ◇ 10 5 3
      ♣ Q 6 5   ♣ Q 7 3 2   ♣ J 9 8 6 3

Hand (9) is not much of a hand, facing a one-level overcall. Nevertheless, you should raise to 2♠. This will deprive the opening bidder of a whole level of bidding. If he does bid, his partner will have to guess whether he has a strong hand or was forced to bid at the three-level because of your raise.

    Hand (10) is much stronger, but if partner holds (say) ♠KQJ64 and a minor-suit king, you would still want to play at the two-level. You show this stronger hand with 2◇, *bidding the opponent's suit*. Whenever you make a bid in the suit opened by an opponent you indicate good values. Here you also show a fit for partner, at least a sound raise to the two-level.

Hand (11) contains four-card spade support and a singleton. To make life even more difficult for your LHO, who is likely to hold a strong hand, you jump to 3♠. Your partner will know that you hold a very weak hand with at least four-card trump support. If you held more points, you would start with a bid of 2♦ instead.

What does it mean if you bid a new suit opposite partner's overcall? The bid is constructive (you should not rescue on a weak hand with a long suit). The simplest method is to play that a response in a new suit is forcing, unless you are a passed hand. It should show 10+ points and a good five-card or longer suit of your own.

Suppose the bidding starts:

LHO	Partner	RHO	You
1♡	2♣	pass	?

and you hold one of these hands:

(12) ♠ A K J 8 3	(13) ♠ A 10 5 4	(14) ♠ 9 3
♡ 9 3	♡ 8 2	♡ 8 7 4
◊ 10 8 5 2	◊ K Q J 8 3	◊ K Q 9 8 6 5 2
♣ Q 6	♣ K 4	♣ 3

With hand (12) there may be a game for your side if your partner has a spade fit, or if he is strong with good clubs. You will respond 2♠, intending to pass a rebid of 3♣ from partner. On hand (13) you hold 13 points and are entitled to respond 2◊. On a sunny day partner may rebid in spades or be able to say 2NT, which you will raise to 3NT.

With hand (14) you will pass. Remember that a response of 2◊ would be constructive, not a rescue. Partner would have to bid again and this might carry you much too high when the two hands fitted together poorly.

Overcalls and responses — Problems A

1. ♠ A J 6 5 ♡ Q 5 4 ◇ A Q J 4 3 ♣ 4

LHO	Partner	RHO	You
		1♡	?

(a) Pass (b) Double (c) 1♠ (d) 2◇

2. ♠ K 10 7 6 2 ♡ 9 5 ◇ 10 8 2 ♣ J 9 6

LHO	Partner	RHO	You
1◇	1♠	2♣	?

(a) Pass (b) 2♠ (c) 3♠ (d) 4♠

3. ♠ K J 9 8 2 ♡ 10 7 ◇ A Q 6 3 ♣ 7 5

LHO	Partner	RHO	You
1♡	1NT	pass	?

What will you bid? What are your future plans?

(a) 2♡ (b) 3♠ (c) 3NT (d) 4♠

4. ♠ A Q 5 ♡ K 10 5 4 ◇ 9 5 ♣ K J 8 6

LHO	Partner	RHO	You
1♠	3◇	pass	?

Neither side is vulnerable. What action will you take?

(a) Pass (b) 3♠ (c) 3NT

5. ♠ A K 10 4 ♡ Q 8 7 ◇ J 9 6 3 ♣ J 3

LHO	Partner	RHO	You
1◇	1♡	pass	?

(a) 1NT (b) 2◇ (c) 2♡ (d) 3♡

(The answers are overleaf.)

Overcalls and responses — Solutions A

1. ♠AJ65 ♡Q54 ◊AQJ43 ♣4

Your RHO opens 1♡. You cannot overcall 1♠ on a four-card suit, and your shape is wrong for a double (no support for clubs). So that leaves either passing or overcalling 2◊. With opening values and a decent diamond suit, 2◊ describes your hand well. **Answer:** (d) 2◊.

2. ♠K 10 7 6 2 ♡9 5 ◊10 8 2 ♣J 9 6

The auction starts: (1◊) - 1♠ - (2♣). With five-card support, you would sometimes go all the way to 4♠. Here you have no side singleton or void and are not worth going that high at any vulnerability. You should bid 3♠, showing a weak hand with good trump support. (With a stronger raise, start with 2◊.) **Answer:** (c) 3♠.

3. ♠KJ982 ♡107 ◊AQ63 ♣75

LHO opens 1♡ and your partner overcalls 1NT. With 10 HCP opposite 15-18, you are worth a game contract. Which game will be better, 3NT or 4♠? You can find out by starting with a transfer response of 2♡, showing at least five spades. Over partner's expected 2♠ you will jump to 3NT. Partner can then choose between the two possible games. **Answer:** (a) 2♡.

4. ♠AQ5 ♡K1054 ◊95 ♣KJ86

With neither side vulnerable LHO opens 1♠ and your partner overcalls 3◊, the next player passing. This is a *weak* jump overcall, remember, and you should pass. Your partner might hold ◊KQJ10732 and little else! In 3NT, the defenders would kill the dummy by holding up the ◊A and you might go four or five down. Suppose instead that partner had overcalled 2◊. Then a game is very possible and you would respond 2NT. Your chances would be better if you held three low diamonds instead of two. **Answer:** (a) Pass.

5. ♠AK104 ♡Q87 ◊J963 ♣J3

Your LHO opens 1◊ and partner overcalls 1♡, next player passing. You are going to show your heart support. Since you have 11 HCP, you begin with 2◊ — a bid in the opponent's suit. This shows at least a sound raise to the two-level (10+). If you were stronger, you could bid 2◊ and then make a further try if partner signed off in 2♡. **Answer:** (b) 2◊.

Overcalls and responses — Problems B

6. ♠ A 10 9 7 5 4   ♡ Q 5 2   ◇ A K   ♣ 8 6

Your RHO opens 1♣ and you overcall 1♠. After a pass by LHO, your partner responds 2♡, the next player passing. What will you say?

    (a) Pass   (b) 2♠   (c) 3♡   (d) 4♡

7. ♠ Q 10 5   ♡ A 9 4   ◇ K 10 5 3   ♣ J 6 4

Your RHO opens 1♡. You pass and so does the next player. Your partner bids 1♠ and the opener passes. What will you say?

    (a) Pass   (b) 1NT   (c) 2♡   (d) 2♠

8. ♠ 6 2   ♡ K 8 5   ◇ Q J 9 3   ♣ A J 10 4

Your LHO opens 1♣ and partner bids 1♠, RHO passing. What will you say?

    (a) Pass   (b) 1NT   (c) 2♣   (d) 2NT

9. ♠ A K 9 7 6 2   ♡ 10 3   ◇ K 5   ♣ A 9 4

Your RHO opens 1◇ and you overcall 1♠. After a pass from LHO your partner responds 2◇. RHO passes. What will you say next?

    (a) 2♠   (b) 2NT   (c) 3♠   (d) 4♠

10. ♠ K Q 6 3   ♡ 9 7   ◇ A J 4   ♣ K 10 9 5

The bidding starts 1◇ - pass - pass. What will you say now?

    (a) Pass   (b) Double   (c) 1♠   (d) 1NT

(The answers are overleaf.)

Overcalls and responses — Solutions B

6.   ♠ A 10 9 7 5 4   ♡ Q 5 2   ◇ A K   ♣ 8 6

The bidding starts

LHO	Partner	RHO	You
		1♣	1♠
pass	2♡	pass	?

Partner's 2♡ is constructive and forcing. You would have to find a second bid even on a minimum overcall with no heart fit. Here you have a respectable hand *and* a fit for partner's hearts! Give partner the good news with a raise all the way to 4♡. Remember you would have to raise to 3♡ if your diamonds were only ◇K4. **Answer:** (d) 4♡.

7.   ♠ Q 10 5   ♡ A 9 4   ◇ K 10 5 3   ♣ J 6 4

Facing a second-seat overcall of 1♠, you would bid 2♡ to show a sound raise to the two-level. When your partner bids in the passout seat, he may well be quite weak. He knows that you hold some points (from his RHO's pass) and he may already be assuming that you have something close to 10 points. In case he does have a good hand (also to shut out your LHO) you should raise to 2♠. You are not quite worth a strength-showing 2♡ instead. **Answer:** (d) 2♠.

8.   ♠ 6 2   ♡ K 8 5   ◇ Q J 9 3   ♣ A J 10 4

The bidding starts 1♣ - 1♠ (by partner) - Pass. Although you hold 11 points, you cannot bid 2♣ because this should show at least three-card support for partner's spades. You are very suitable for a response in notrump. If partner held the values for an opening bid, on some different sequence, you might bid 2NT to suggest a game. Here he has only overcalled at the one-level and may hold no more than 8 or 9 points. Respond just 1NT, suggesting around 8-11 HCP. With 12-14 HCP, you would go to 2NT. **Answer:** (b) 1NT.

9.   ♠ A K 9 7 6 2   ♡ 10 3   ◇ K 5   ♣ A 9 4

The bidding starts 1◇ - 1♠ (by you) - Pass - 2◇. The next player passes and you must calculate your rebid. Partner has shown (at least) a sound raise to 2♠. You have six excellent trumps and two good cards outside. You should bid 4♠ now. A jump to 3♠ would not be forcing and you might miss an excellent game. **Answer:** (d) 4♠.

10. ♠K Q 6 3 ♡9 7 ◇A J 4 ♣K 10 9 5

The bidding starts 1◇ - Pass - Pass. You cannot double because you have no support for hearts. Nor is an overcall of 1♠ a good bid, when you have only four cards in the suit. Your hand would be too weak for a 1NT overcall in second seat (you would have to pass, in fact). In the fourth seat, the balancing or passout seat, a 1NT overcall shows around 12-14 points. This is the action you should take. **Answer:** (d) 1NT.

10

TAKEOUT DOUBLES AND RESPONSES

Early in the auction, the most common meaning of a double is to ask partner to choose a trump suit (or notrump), and also to give some idea as to the strength of his hand. In other words, it is a **takeout double**. The doubler's partner is not expected to pass, as he would if it was a penalty double; he is expected to bid. All the doubles below are for takeout:

	WEST	NORTH	EAST	SOUTH
(1)			1♡	dbl
(2)	1♠	pass	pass	dbl
(3)			3♣	dbl
(4)	1◇	pass	3◇	dbl
(5)	1♣	pass	1♠	dbl

In sequence (1), South doubles 1♡ to ask partner to choose one of the other three suits (or notrump). For example, North might respond 1♠, showing that he would like to choose spades as trumps. Also, because he responded at the minimum level he would tell the doubler that he is not particularly strong — about 0-7 points.

In sequence (2), South's double after two passes is again for takeout. The best way to enter the auction over opening weak two-bids and weak three-bids is usually a takeout double. In sequence (3), that is the action chosen by South. In sequence (4), South makes a takeout double of 3◇. Now if North holds length in hearts, for example, he will usually respond either 3♡ or 4♡ depending on the strength of his hand. The opponents have bid two suits in auction (5). South doubles, asking partner to choose one of the unbid suits

What strength does a takeout double show?

As a general rule, a takeout double shows at least the values for an opening bid. When you have near-perfect shape (shortage in the suit they have bid and support for the other three suits), you can double on 13 points or more — remember to add dummy points, as most of the time you will be dummy. When your shape is worse, you will need more points.

Suppose your right-hand opponent (RHO) has opened 1♠ and you are considering a takeout double on one of these hands:

(1)	♠ 10	(2)	♠ A 3	(3)	♠ K 8
	♡ A Q 9 3		♡ K 7 2		♡ A K J 2
	◇ Q 8 5		◇ K Q 9 6		◇ A K 10 7 3
	♣ K J 7 6 2		♣ K 7 5 2		♣ 8 2

Hand (1) has only 12 HCP but good shape for a takeout double. In particular, you hold four cards in hearts, the unbid major. Hand (2) does not contain four cards in the unbid major, and with 15 points you should probably choose a 1NT overcall rather than a double, although you would like to have a little more in spades. Hand (3) does not contain satisfactory support for clubs, one of the three unbid suits. However, if partner responds 2♣, you are strong enough to continue with 2◇. You show a good hand (18+ HCP) when you double and then bid a new suit after partner's response.

Responding to a takeout double

When partner makes a takeout double, you have two duties to perform. You must choose a trump suit (or notrump). You must also give some indication of the strength of your hand. Suppose partner has doubled 1◇ for takeout. These are your main options in response:

1♡/1♠/2♣	About 0-8 points
1NT	8-10 HCP and a diamond stopper
2◇	Artificial, showing 10+ points
2♡/2♠/3♣	9-11 points
2NT	11-12 HCP and a diamond stopper
game bids	to play

All the point-counts are approximate, since you can assign extra value to a responding hand that contains a long suit or other good distribution. Let's look at some examples. The bidding starts:

West	North	East	South
1♦	dbl	pass	?

and you must find a response on one of these South hands:

(4) ♠ Q 10 7 6	(5) ♠ A Q 7 6	(6) ♠ K Q 10 5
♡ 9 8 3	♡ K 7	♡ 9 6
◇ 10 8 5 4	◇ 9 6 3	◇ J 6 5
♣ J 6	♣ 10 9 5 4	♣ A Q 8 2

Hand (4) is very weak, yes, but you are forced to make a response. It would be a horrible mistake to pass. You expect your partner to be short in diamonds and declarer would surely make his contract of 1◇ doubled. You respond 1♠, saying that you think spades will be the best trump suit and that you hold 0-8 points.

Hand (5) is much stronger, with 9 HCP. Let partner know this! You respond 2♠, suggesting 9-11 points. By giving partner an accurate idea of your strength, you make it easier for him to judge whether a game contract will be possible.

Hand (6) is even stronger and you have a good chance of making a game contract. You show your strength (11+ points) by *bidding the opponent's suit*. You respond 2◇. You and your partner will then bid your suits, looking for a fit. If he says 2♡ next, for example, you will bid 2♠. Do not think that bidding the opponent's suit is too difficult or complicated for you. We have already encountered it in Chapter 9, where it was used to show good support for partner's overcall. It is an essential part of bidding in many other circumstances too, as we will see in later chapters.

Sometimes you find yourself in an awkward situation, with no suit to bid. Suppose your partner has doubled the opening bid of 1♡ and you hold one of these hands:

(7) ♠ 7 6 4	(8) ♠ 10 3	(9) ♠ 5 2	(10) ♠ A Q 10 6 4
♡ J 9 8 3	♡ K 10 9 5 2	♡ K Q J 10 6	♡ 3 2
◇ 9 7 3	◇ Q J 6	◇ 10 6 5	◇ K Q J
♣ J 7 2	♣ Q 4 3	♣ A 9 6	♣ 4 3 2

Again, do not pass (or even think of passing) on hand (7)! Declarer is very likely to make 1♡ doubled, probably with an overtrick or so. Respond 1♠, keeping the bidding low. It is not your fault that you have an awful hand and no four-card suit to show. Bid your cheapest three-card suit — partner will understand later!

On hand (8), again you should not pass. You will respond 1NT, suggesting 8-10 HCP.

Only when you have a solid holding in the opponent's suit, as on hand (9), are you entitled to pass the takeout double for penalties. Your partner will then usually do best to lead a trump, so that you can start to draw their trumps. In order to pass partner's takeout double, you need three sure trump tricks and an outside trick.

On hand (10) you have 13 points including distribution and should simply jump to 4♠, knowing partner has adequate support for all three unbid suits.

Takeout doubles of preemptive openings

A few decades back, there was a splendid array of different methods for bidding over a preemptive opening. Nowadays, players have seen the light and almost everyone uses the method that is easily best — a takeout double! All bids in a new suit are natural, and so is an overcall of 3NT.

Suppose your LHO opens 3◊, partner doubles for takeout and the next player passes. What would you say on each of these hands?

(11)	♠ 10 8 4	(12)	♠ A Q 10 3	(13)	♠ A J 8 7 3
	♡ K 9 7 6		♡ K 10 8 4		♡ 10 7
	◊ Q 7		◊ 8 2		◊ 10 5
	♣ K 8 6 2		♣ Q 4 3		♣ K 10 8 5

On hand (11) you hold four cards in an unbid major, so you are obviously happy to respond in hearts. Should you bid 3♡ or 4♡? Your partner will already be expecting you to hold a few points. Here you have no more than he will expect and should respond only 3♡. You cannot expect the ◊Q to be very useful, so your hand is not really worth more than about 6 points.

On hand (12) you have enough to justify a game contract, but should you bid 4♡ or 4♠? There is no need to guess. Remember that when you bid the opponent's suit opposite a double or an overcall, this shows a strong hand. You respond 4◊, passing the message: 'I have a good hand. Let's look for a trump fit.' Your partner will probably bid 4♡ or 4♠. You will then pass, knowing that you have found a 4-4 fit. This is way better than your having to guess whether to bid 4♡ or 4♠. You might then end up in a 4-3 fit.

Hand (13) contains only 8 points, but they are all 'working', as players say. What is more, you have a five-card major! That is worth an extra 2 points or so. Bid 4♠.

Following up your takeout double

You enter the auction with a takeout double and hear partner's response. What then? With close to a minimum double, you will usually pass. With extra values, you may be able to bid a game or make a game try. Suppose the opening bid is 1♢ and you double on one of the following hands. What are your future bidding plans?

(14)	♠ A 10 7 6	(15)	♠ K J 4	(16)	♠ A Q 8 7
	♡ K 8 7 6		♡ A Q 10 2		♡ A K 10 6
	♢ K 2		♢ 9 6		♢ 10
	♣ Q 5 2		♣ A 9 7 3		♣ A 10 6 5

Look at hand (14) first. You double RHO's 1♢. If partner responds 1♡, 1♠ or 2♣, you will pass (with better shape — say a singleton diamond — you could raise a 1♡ response to 2♡). What if partner responds 2♡, 2♠ or 3♣? Again you will pass. Remember that these single-jump responses are non-forcing. They show around 9-11 points and your hand is not likely to yield a game. If instead partner responds with a 2♢ cuebid, you will bid 2♡. The bidding will then continue until a fit is found.

Hand (15) is stronger. You would still pass a response of 1♡, 1♠ or 2♣. If partner bids 2♡ (9-11 points), you would make a game try of 3♡. If instead he bids 2♠ or 3♣, game would still be unlikely and you would pass.

Finally, we look at hand (16) where you have 17 HCP and better shape. If partner responded 1♡ or 1♠, you would raise to 3♡ or 3♠. You would raise 2♣ to 3♣. If partner made a single jump to 2♡, 2♠ or 3♣, you would head for game.

Takeout Doubles and Responses — Problems A

1.   ♠ A Q 9 8 2 ♡ Q 5 ◇ K 10 5 ♣ Q 9 3

Your RHO opens 1♠. What will you say?

    (a) Pass   (b) Dbl   (c) 1NT

2.   ♠ A K 9 2 ♡ A J 10 7 6 ◇ J 6 3 ♣ 6

West	North	East	South
1♣	pass	1◇	?

    (a) Pass   (b) Dbl   (c) 1♡

3.   ♠ 6 2 ♡ A Q 10 7 3 ◇ K 10 9 5 ♣ A 2

West	North	East	South
1♡	pass	2♡	?

    (a) Pass   (b) Dbl   (c) 3◇

4.   ♠ A 9 ♡ A J 5 3 ◇ 10 9 6 3 ♣ 6 4 2

West	North	East	South
1◇	dbl	pass	?

    (a) Pass   (b) 1♡   (c) 2♡

5.   ♠ 9 ♡ A K J 4 ◇ A Q 7 6 3 ♣ K 4 2

West	North	East	South
1♠	pass	3♠	?

    (a) Pass   (b) Dbl   (c) 4◇   (d) 4♡

(The answers are overleaf.)

Takeout Doubles and Responses — Solutions A

1.   ♠ A Q 9 8 2   ♡ Q 5   ◇ K 10 5   ♣ Q 9 3

Your RHO opens 1♠. A double would be for takeout and partner's most likely response would be 2♡, where you have no support. You are not strong enough for a 1NT overcall, which would show 15-18 HCP. You should pass. **Answer:** (a) Pass.

2.   ♠ A K 9 2   ♡ A J 10 7 6   ◇ J 6 3   ♣ 6

The bidding starts (1♣) - Pass - (1◇) to you. You have enough to contest the auction. With support for both the unbid suits, it is best to double. If partner holds the same length in both majors, he will respond 1♡ (the cheaper suit) and you will be in your best fit. It would not be so good to overcall 1♡, guessing that this is the best trump suit. Partner might hold only one heart and four or five spades. **Answer:** (b) Dbl.

3.   ♠ 6 2   ♡ A Q 10 7 3   ◇ K 10 9 5   ♣ A 2

The auction goes (1♡) - Pass - (2♡) to you. You cannot contemplate a double because it would be for takeout. Your partner would almost certainly respond in one of the black suits, where you hold no support. Not only would you probably end in a silly contract, you would have let the opponents off the hook. They are heading for an awful heart break and will not relish playing their final contract, whatever it should be. Of course, 3◇ on a four-card suit is obviously wrong. **Answer:** (a) Pass.

4.   ♠ A 9   ♡ A J 5 3   ◇ 10 9 6 3   ♣ 6 4 2

Your LHO opens 1◇ and partner doubles for takeout. The next player passes and you now have two duties: to choose a trump suit (or notrump) and to give an idea of your strength. Here you want to suggest hearts as trumps. Should you respond 1♡ or 2♡? You would have to bid 1♡ on this shape even if you held only 1 or 2 points. You should respond 2♡, telling partner that you hold around 9-11 points. **Answer:** (c) 2♡.

5.   ♠ 9   ♡ A K J 4   ◇ A Q 7 6 3   ♣ K 4 2

The bidding is (1♠) - Pass - (3♠) to you. With this number of points and support for all three unbid suits, you have enough for a takeout double. Overcalling 4◇ would not be a good bid. Partner might have no diamond support at all, so it is better to ask him to choose a suit. **Answer:** (b) Dbl.

Takeout Doubles and Responses — Problems B

6. ♠ 9 8 4 2   ♡ Q 5 2   ◇ 10 7 3   ♣ J 9 2

West	North	East	South
1♠	dbl	pass	?

(a) Pass   (b) 1NT   (c) 2♣   (d) 2♡

7. ♠ Q 7 5 2   ♡ A Q 9 4   ◇ A 10 5   ♣ J 6

West	North	East	South
1◇	dbl	pass	?

(a) 2◇   (b) 2♡   (c) 3NT   (d) 4♡

8. ♠ A Q 8 7 3   ♡ K 5   ◇ K 9 4   ♣ 9 7 6

West	North	East	South
1♣	dbl	pass	?

(a) 1♠   (b) 2♣   (c) 2♠   (d) 4♠

9. ♠ K 6   ♡ 9 8 4   ◇ A Q 6 5   ♣ J 9 8 3

West	North	East	South
1◇	dbl	pass	?

(a) Pass   (b) 1NT   (c) 2♣   (d) 3♣

10. ♠ A K 10 8   ♡ A 9 7   ◇ 7 3   ♣ A Q 10 3

West	North	East	South
		1◇	dbl
pass	1♠	pass	?

(a) Pass   (b) 1NT   (c) 2♠   (d) 3♠

(The answers are overleaf.)

Takeout Doubles and Responses — Solutions B

6.   ♠9 8 4 2   ♡Q 5 2   ◇10 7 3   ♣J 9 2

The bidding starts (1♠) - dbl - (pass). That's awkward! You have no unbid suit containing four cards or more. Responding 1NT would be poor.: you do not have a stopper in spades, and you are well short of 6-9 HCP that such a response requires. Just look for the lowest bid possible. Here you respond 2♣ and hope for the best. It's not *your* fault that you were dealt such a poor hand! **Answer:** (c) *2♣*.

7.   ♠Q 7 5 2   ♡A Q 9 4   ◇A 10 5   ♣J 6

The bidding starts (1◇) - dbl - (pass). You are strong enough to insist on game, but which game? A response of 2♡ would not do your hand justice: it would suggest only 9-11 points and be non-forcing. If you bid 3NT, 4♡ or 4♠, you are trying to guess the best game. The right option, by a mile, is a cuebid of 2◇. If partner bids 2♡ or 2♠, you can then raise to game in that suit. In the unlikely event that he has no four-card major, you will play in 3NT. **Answer:** (a) 2◇.

8.   ♠A Q 8 7 3   ♡K 5   ◇K 9 4   ♣9 7 6

The bidding starts (1♣) - dbl (by partner) - (pass). You are happy to make spades trumps, so you must judge how many spades to bid. 1♠ would be a bad underbid; you would have to bid 1♠ on some hands with no points at all. 2♠ would also be an underbid, showing around 9-11 points. With five cards in a major suit, where you expect partner to hold support, you are worth closer to 14 points than 12 points. You should go all the way to 4♠. **Answer:** (d) 4♠.

9.   ♠K 6   ♡9 8 4   ◇A Q 6 5   ♣J 9 8 3

The bidding starts (1◇) - dbl - (pass). If you were going to respond in clubs, you would bid 3♣ (9-11 points) rather than 2♣ (0-7 points). However, with your double stopper in diamonds it is much better to respond 1NT. If your partner has a good hand it is much more likely that the possible game will be 3NT than 5♣. **Answer:** (b) 1NT.

10.   ♠A K 10 8   ♡A 9 7   ◇7 3   ♣A Q 10 3

The bidding starts (1◇) - dbl (by you) - (pass) - 1♠ - (pass). Although partner has denied the values for 2♠, you might still make game. You are worth a raise to 2♠. If partner has around 6-7 points, he may advance towards 4♠. For example, game would be good opposite: ♠Q975 ♡J4 ◇1086 ♣KJ64. **Answer:** (c) 2♠.

Takeout Doubles and Responses – Problems C

11.   ♠ K J 8 2 ♡ 6 ◊ 8 7 5 ♣ A Q 10 7 2

Your LHO opens 1◊, partner doubles and the next player bids 3◊. What will you say?

    (a) 3♠   (b) 4♣   (c) 4◊   (d) 4♠   (e) 5♣

12.   ♠ A J 5 4 ♡ K Q 10 7 ◊ J 2 ♣ A 10 6

West	North	East	South
1◊	pass	1NT	?

    (a) Pass   (b) Dbl   (c) 2♡   (d) 2♠

13.   ♠ A 8 6 ♡ A Q 7 6 ◊ 9 ♣ K J 7 5 2

West	North	East	South
		1◊	dbl
pass	2♡	pass	?

    (a) Pass   (b) 3♡   (c) 4♡

14.   ♠ A 7 ♡ A Q 7 6 ◊ A K J 6 5 ♣ 6 3

West	North	East	South
		1♣	dbl
pass	1♠	pass	?

    (a) Pass   (b) 2♣   (c) 2◊   (d) 3◊

15.   ♠ A K 10 8 ♡ A 9 7 ◊ K 10 3 ♣ A J 7

West	North	East	South
		1♣	dbl
pass	1♡	pass	?

    (a) Pass   (b) 1♠   (c) 1NT   (d) 2♣   (e) 2♡

(The answers are overleaf.)

Takeout Doubles and Responses — Solutions C

11. ♠ K J 8 2 ♡ 6 ◇ 8 7 5 ♣ A Q 10 7 2

The bidding starts (1◇) - dbl - (3◇). You have enough to attempt a game in one of the black suits. How can you choose between 4♠ and 5♣? If you bid either black suit, you are simply guessing. Instead you should show your strength with 4◇. Partner will bid his cheapest suit. If he bids 4♠, you have found a fit. If instead he bids 4♡, you will bid 4♠. With five spades you would have been willing to bid 4♠ straight away. So, partner can infer that you have four spades and probably five clubs. **Answer:** (c) 4◇.

12. ♠ A J 5 4 ♡ K Q 10 7 ◇ J 2 ♣ A 10 6

The bidding starts (1◇) - pass - (1NT). If you chose to bid 2♡ or 2♠ now, you would be showing at least a five-card suit. You are strong enough to contest the auction and it is quite likely that partner will have length in one of the unbid suits. You should make a takeout double. Everyone treats a double in this auction as a takeout double of diamonds. You are prepared for any response that your partner might make. **Answer:** (b) Dbl.

13. ♠ A 8 6 ♡ A Q 7 6 ◇ 9 ♣ K J 7 5 2

Your RHO opens 1◇. You double and partner responds 2♡. This suggests 9-11 points and is non-forcing. You have a bit to spare and do have four-card heart support. You are worth a game try of 3♡ but no more. **Answer:** (b) 3♡.

14. ♠ A 7 ♡ A Q 7 6 ◇ A K J 6 5 ♣ 6 3

The bidding starts (1♣) - dbl (by you) - (pass) - 1♠ - (pass). Judging that your hand is too strong for a 1◇ overcall, you begin with a double. Partner responds 1♠ and the opponents are silent. You should bid 2◇ now. By changing the suit after a takeout double you show a powerful hand (18+ HCP). Remember that partner was forced to bid and might have no values at all. **Answer:** (c) 2◇.

15. ♠ A K 10 8 ♡ A 9 7 ◇ K 10 3 ♣ A J 7

Your RHO opens 1♣. You are too strong to overcall 1NT so you begin with a takeout double. Your partner responds 1♡, with the opponents not bidding again. You can show your strength by bidding 1NT now. An original 1NT overcall would have shown around 15-18 HCP, and with 13-14 HCP you would pass partner's 1♡ bid, so 1NT after an initial double suggests 19-21 HCP. **Answer:** (c) 1NT.

11

WHEN THEY DOUBLE OR OVERCALL

Players are keen to get into the auction nowadays and many auctions are contested. In this chapter we will look at the best tactics when your partner has opened and the next player competes, either with a takeout double or an overcall.

What to do when your RHO makes a takeout double

Partner opens 1♡ and the next player doubles. These are your main options:

Redouble	10+ HCP, fewer than four hearts
1♠	Natural and forcing
1NT	7-9 HCP, balanced
2♣/2♢	Natural and non-forcing
2♡	Three-card support, 6-9 points
2NT	10+ with at least four-card support
3♡/4♡	Preemptive

When you have a moderate hand with four-card support for partner, it is essential that you take away the opponents' bidding space by bidding as high as possible. Suppose the bidding starts 1♡ - (dbl) and you hold one of these hands:

(1)	♠ 9 6	(2)	♠ 9 8 2	(3)	♠ K 8
	♡ K 10 4		♡ A 8 7 3		♡ Q J 9 2
	♢ Q 10 8 5		♢ Q 10 5 4		♢ 9 7 3
	♣ J 9 8 3		♣ 10 4		♣ A 10 9 2

On hand (1) you raise to 2♡, just as you would without the double. On hand (2), with four-card support, you jump to 3♡, making life difficult for the next player. Although you have to make some allowance for the vulnerability, the general rule on deals where the points are fairly evenly distributed is that you should...

Raise to the level dictated by your side's combined trump length.

Look back at hands (1) and (2) above. With the first hand you expect the combined trump length to be 5+3=8. You therefore raise to the eight-trick level (2♡). On (2), expecting nine trumps, you raise to 3♡. Don't worry that partner will think you have a better hand when you bid 3♡. This is known to be a preemptive bid. If you had a sound raise to the three-level, such as hand (3), you would bid 2NT.

After an intervening double, a new suit is forcing at the one-level and non-forcing at the two-level. Suppose your partner opens 1◊ and the next player doubles. You hold one of these hands:

(4) ♠ J 4	(5) ♠ 7 6	(6) ♠ K 5 3
♡ A J 10 7 6	♡ K 7	♡ A 10 4
◊ K 10 5	◊ 9 6 3	◊ 10 6 5
♣ J 6 3	♣ A Q 8 7 4 2	♣ Q 9 8 2

Do not waste time with a redouble on (4) – you have no interest in doubling a spade contract. Bid a forcing 1♡, just as you would have done without the double, and continue to bid constructively thereafter. On (5) you are glad you can introduce your handsome club suit by bidding 2♣. This suggests around 7-11 points and is non-forcing. If you held another king, you would start with a redouble instead, bidding clubs at your next turn. With hand (6) you should respond 1NT. There are two good reasons for this. Firstly, you prevent a one-level response from the next player. Secondly, you allow your partner to contest the auction subsequently when he has shape but not enough points to bid on his own.

What to do when your RHO makes an overcall

When the second player has overcalled instead of doubling, you will again think about bidding as high as possible when you have a good trump fit for partner. With no fit, you have an additional option – double. For all modern players this double is is for takeout, shows interest in any unbid major(s), and asks partner to continue to describe his hand. It is called a **negative double**. If the overcall is higher than 3♠, however, a double is for penalties.

Suppose your partner opens 1◊ and the next player overcalls 1♠. These are your main options:

Double	A negative double, guaranteeing four hearts
1NT	7-9 HCP, balanced with a spade stopper
2♣	four+ cards, natural and forcing, 10+ points
2◊	Weak raise of diamonds, 6-9 points
2♡	five+ cards, natural and forcing, 10+ points
2♠	Strong raise of diamonds, 10+ points
3◊	Preemptive raise of diamonds

After a start of 1◊ - 1♠ (by RHO), you hold one of these hands:

(7)	♠ 10 3	(8)	♠ 7 4	(9)	♠ 10 5 2
	♡ A Q 8 3		♡ A K 10 4 3		♡ 8
	◊ 9 7 3		◊ Q 7 6		◊ K 10 6 5 4
	♣ Q J 7 4		♣ K 10 5		♣ Q 9 6 4

On (7) you make a negative double (for takeout). On this auction you will nearly always hold at least four cards in hearts. On (8) you bid a forcing 2♡ – there is no need to make a negative double when you have a perfectly good natural bid available to describe your hand. With (9) you raise preemptively to 3◊. If instead you held a sound raise to 3◊ (10+ points), you would bid 2♠ instead. Remember that a bid in the opponents' suit always shows strength.

Which suit(s) does a negative double show?

The suit or suits shown by a negative double vary according to the suits that have been bid by the first two players. Most of the time the doubler will hold any unbid major suits.

West	North	East	South
1♣	1◊	dbl	

Sitting West, you can expect East to hold at least four-plus cards in both hearts and spades — a hand such as:

♠ K J 6 2   ♡ A 10 7 4   ◊ 8 6 3   ♣ Q 5

If he held four cards in one major and fewer in the other, perhaps:

♠ K 7 6   ♡ A K 7 2   ◊ 8 7 3   ♣ 10 5 2

he would simply bid his four-card major at the one-level (here he would bid 1♡).

West	North	East	South
1♣	1♡	dbl	

Here East almost certainly holds four spades. If he held five or more spades, he would respond 1♠ instead.

West	North	East	South
1◊	2♣	dbl	

This is a tricky start to the auction for East. A 2♡ or 2♠ bid would show five-plus cards in the suit bid. So, East will be forced to double when he holds some points and only one four-card major, a hand such as:

♠ A J 7 6 ♡ Q 7 2 ◇ K 6 3 ♣ 10 9 5

The opener may then have an awkward rebid. This is why players like to overcall 2♣ over 1◇. It takes away quite a bit of bidding space from the opponents.

What happens when you want to make a penalty double?

Since a direct double of an overcall is a negative double (for takeout), you may wonder what happens when you hold a hand on which you would like to have made a penalty double. This deal illustrates the situation:

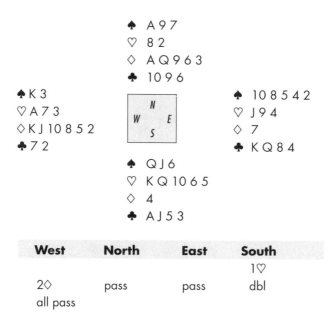

West	North	East	South
			1♡
2◇	pass	pass	dbl
all pass			

As North, you would have liked to make a penalty double of 2◇ but nowadays such doubles are for takeout. You have to pass instead. East passes and your partner then has a chance to say something. Whenever he holds two or fewer diamonds, he should consider balancing with a takeout double. East did not raise diamonds, so it is quite likely that you have good diamonds sitting over the 2◇ bidder.

When this is the case, you pass the takeout double. On this deal you will pick up a substantial penalty. (If you did not hold good diamonds, you would make some other response to partner's balancing double.) In this way you get the considerable advantages of playing negative doubles without having to wave goodbye to the available penalties when you hold a trump stack over the overcaller.

When they double or overcall - Problems A

1.   ♠9 ♡10 9 6 5 ◇A Q 7 6 3 ♣10 8 4

Your partner opens 1♠ and the next player doubles. What action will you take?

    (a) Pass   (b) Redbl   (c) 1NT   (d) 2◇

2.   ♠Q 9 8 6 2 ♡K 5 4 ◇10 5 ♣J 9 2

Your partner opens 1♡ and the next player bids 2♣. What will you say?

    (a) Pass   (b) Dbl   (c) 2♡   (d) 2♠

3.   ♠10 9 6 3 ♡A Q 10 7 6 ◇Q 6 ♣A J

The bidding starts 1♡ (from you) - 2◇ - Dbl - Pass. What will you say?

    (a) Pass   (b) 2♡   (c) 2♠

4.   ♠K 8 7 2 ♡10 9 2 ◇7 6 4 ♣A K 4

Your partner opens 1♠ and the next player doubles. What will you say?

    (a) Redbl   (b) 2♠   (c) 2NT   (d) 3♠

5.   ♠A K 4 ♡Q 10 5 3 ◇6 4 ♣Q 9 6 2

Your partner opens 1◇ and the next player doubles. What will you say on this hand?

    (a) Redbl   (b) 1♡   (c) 2NT

(The answers are overleaf.)

When they double or overcall — Solutions A

1.   ♠9   ♡10 9 6 5   ◇A Q 7 6 3   ♣10 8 4

Partner opens 1♠ and the next player doubles. Without the double you would have responded 1NT, keeping the bidding alive in case partner had a good hand. When there is an intervening double, partner will have a second chance to bid on a good hand. Anyway, 1NT here would show 7-9 HCP. You are unsuitable for 2◇; your suit is not good enough and your hand is too weak. **Answer:** (a) Pass.

2.   ♠Q 9 8 6 2   ♡K 5 4   ◇10 5   ♣J 9 2

Partner opens 1♡ and the next player overcalls 2♣. You should raise to 2♡, just as you would have done if your RHO had passed. By showing your support, you will enable partner to bid higher in hearts, either to contest the auction further if the opponents bid again or to look for a heart game. **Answer:** (c) 2♡.

3.   ♠10 9 6 3   ♡A Q 10 7 6   ◇Q 6   ♣A J

You open 1♡, LHO overcalls 2◇ and your partner doubles. This is a negative double — a takeout double. Your partner almost certainly holds four cards in spades, the unbid major, and you should respond 2♠. If you held the ♠K instead of the ♠10, you would be strong enough to respond 3♠. It's the same situation as when you respond to a normal takeout double: not only must you choose a trump suit (or notrump), you must also give some indication of your strength. Partner can then judge if a game contract will be a good idea. **Answer:** (c) 2♠.

4.   ♠K 8 7 2   ♡10 9 2   ◇7 6 4   ♣A K 4

Partner opens 1♠ and the next player doubles. Your hand is worth a sound raise to 3♠ and that is what you would have bid if the next player had passed. Over a double this response would be preemptive, showing a weak hand with four spades. To tell partner that you have a sound double raise with four trumps, you make the artificial bid of 2NT instead. **Answer:** (c) 2NT.

5.   ♠A K 4   ♡Q 10 5 3   ◇6 4   ♣Q 9 6 2

Your partner opens 1◇ and the next player doubles. A response of 1♡ would be forcing but it's not particularly attractive since there is a good chance that the doubler holds four hearts. You cannot bid 2NT because this would be an artificial bid that showed a sound raise to at least 3◇. Instead you should redouble to tell partner that you hold at least 10 points and are interested in a possible penalty double of the opponents' resting spot. **Answer:** (a) Redouble.

When they double or overcall — Problems B

6.   ♠J 8 4   ♡ 2   ◇A 10 8 4   ♣A Q 9 5 2

Partner opens 1♡ and your RHO overcalls 2♣. What will you say?

    (a) Pass   (b) Dbl   (c) 2NT

7.   ♠J 7 5   ♡A K Q 9 4   ◇10 3   ♣A 9 6

You open 1♡ and your LHO overcalls 2◇. Partner bids 2♠ and the next player passes. What will you say?

    (a) Pass   (b) 3♡   (c) 3♠   (d) 4♠

8.   ♠A 8 6   ♡A K J 4   ◇7 3   ♣Q J 6 5

Your partner opens 1◇ and the next player overcalls 1♠. What will you say?

    (a) Dbl   (b) 2♣   (c) 2♡   (d) 3NT

9.   ♠A Q 7 6 2   ♡6 4   ◇A 9 7 3   ♣A 10

The bidding starts 1♠ (from you) - Dbl - 3♠ - Pass. What will you say now?

    (a) Pass   (b) 4♠

10.   ♠Q 10 8 4   ♡9 7 2   ◇A Q J 6   ♣K 7

The bidding starts 1◇ - 1♡ - Dbl (by partner) - 2♡. What will you say now?

    (a) Pass   (b) 2♠   (c) 3◇

(The answers are overleaf.)

When they double or overcall — Solutions B

6.   ♠J84 ♡2 ♢A 10 8 4 ♣A Q 9 5 2

The bidding starts 1♡ (from partner) - 2♣. You would like to double for penalties but a double would be negative (for takeout). If you bid 2NT, to show 11-12 HCP and a good club stopper, there is no guarantee that you will end up making a game somewhere. Meanwhile, you will have waved goodbye to a considerable penalty. Your best move is to pass, hoping that your partner will reopen with a double. He is almost certain to do this since he must be short in clubs. You will pass the double and collect a big penalty. **Answer:** (a) Pass.

7.   ♠J75 ♡A K Q 9 4 ♢10 3 ♣A 9 6

You open 1♡ and the next player overcalls 2♢. Partner responds 2♠ and your RHO passes. Partner has made a forcing bid and will hold five-plus spades and at least 10 or 11 points. You have a good hand in support of spades, offering partner several tricks in hearts, the ♣A and a possible ruffing value in diamonds. You are well worth a raise to 4♠. **Answer:** (d) 4♠.

8.   ♠A 8 6 ♡A K J 4 ♢7 3 ♣Q J 6 5

Partner opens 1♢ and the next player overcalls 1♠. Since you have no five-card suit to bid, you should start with a negative double. Although you might hold only 8 points or so for such a call, you can also make a negative double on stronger hands. You plan to bid again, of course, once you have heard partner's response. **Answer:** (a) Dbl.

9.   ♠A Q 7 6 2 ♡6 4 ♢A 9 7 3 ♣A 10

You open 1♠, the next player doubles and partner raises to 3♠. This is a weak preemptive bid. You can expect your partner to hold four spades to the king and perhaps a king or queen outside. You would bid game over a normal 3♠ raise without the intervening double, yes, but partner does not hold such a hand. He is bidding high to shut out the opponents. You should pass. **Answer:** (a) Pass.

10.   ♠Q 10 8 4 ♡9 7 2 ♢A Q J 6 ♣K 7

The bidding starts 1♢ - 1♡ - Dbl (by partner) - 2♡. You can expect partner to hold four spades. (With five spades he would have responded 1♠ instead of making a negative double). You have a fair hand in support of spades and should not allow yourself to be shut out by this heart raise. **Answer:** (b) 2♠.

When they double or overcall — Problems C

11.   ♠ A J 8 4   ♡ Q 7 4   ◇ A 10 9 2   ♣ 9 5

Partner opens 1◇ and your RHO overcalls 2♣. What will you say?

     (a) Dbl   (b) 2♠   (c) 3♣   (d) 3◇

12.   ♠ Q 9 8 3   ♡ 10 5 4   ◇ A 3   ♣ A Q 10 6

You open 1♣, the next player overcalls 1◇ and partner bids 1♠. What will you say when the next player raises to 3◇?

     (a) Pass   (b) Dbl   (c) 3♠   (d) 3NT

13.   ♠ J 2   ♡ J 8 6 4   ◇ K 10 9 6 5   ♣ 10 7

Your partner opens 1◇ and the next player doubles. What will you say?

     (a) Pass   (b) 1♡   (c) 2◇   (d) 3◇

14.   ♠ 9 6 2   ♡ K 10 8 7   ◇ A 9 3   ♣ A 10 4

Partner opens 1♣ and the next player overcalls 1♠. You make a negative double, the next player passes and partner rebids 2♡. What action will you take?

     (a) Pass   (b) 2♠   (c) 3♡

15.   ♠ Q 10 7 3   ♡ J 9 7 6   ◇ K 8 2   ♣ A 7

Partner opens 1◇ and the next player overcalls 2♣. You make a negative double, the next player passing, and partner rebids 2NT. What will you say next?

     (a) Pass   (b) 3♣   (c) 3◇   (d) 3NT

(The answers are overleaf.)

When they double or overcall — Solutions C

11.   ♠ A J 8 4   ♡ Q 7 4   ◇ A 10 9 2   ♣ 9 5

Partner opens 1◇ and the next player overcalls 2♣. You cannot bid 2♠ because this would show at least a five-card suit. You could bid 3♣ to show a sound raise to (at least) 3◇, but you might then miss a fit in spades. The best idea is to start with a negative double, in the hope that partner will bid spades. If he doesn't, you can support diamonds. **Answer:** (a) Dbl.

12.   ♠ Q 9 8 3   ♡ 10 5 4   ◇ A 3   ♣ A Q 10 6

You open 1♣, the next player overcalls 1◇ and partner bids 1♠. Your RHO raises preemptively to 3◇. What now? If RHO had passed or bid just 2◇, you would have raised to 2♠. This option has been removed by the opponents, so you have to choose between a Pass and raising to 3♠. You should show the spade support. Partner may well hold five spades on this bidding, giving you a nine-card fit. He will realize that you may have been forced to stretch a bit by the 3◇ raise. **Answer:** (c) 3♠.

13.   ♠ J 2   ♡ J 8 6 4   ◇ K 10 9 6 5   ♣ 10 7

Partner opens 1◇ and the next player doubles. There are several reasons why it is wrong to bid 1♡ now. You suit is weak and there is a good chance that the doubler holds four hearts. To make it harder for the opponents to find their likely spade fit, you want to take away bidding space. You should raise preemptively to 3◇. This will prevent the fourth player from bidding 1♠ or 2♠. If he ventures a bid of 3♠, his partner will not know if he was full value for the bid or if he was forced to stretch a bit by your 3◇. **Answer:** (d) 3◇.

14.   ♠ 9 6 2   ♡ K 10 8 7   ◇ A 9 3   ♣ A 10 4

The bidding starts 1♣ (from partner), 1♠ overcall and a negative double from you. The next player passes and your partner rebids 2♡. Even though your hand has 4-3-3-3 shape, you are just about worth a game try. You should invite game by raising to 3♡. **Answer:** (c) 3♡.

15.   ♠ Q 10 7 3   ♡ J 9 7 6   ◇ K 8 2   ♣ A 7

Partner opens 1◇ and the next player overcalls 2♣. You double, the next player passes and partner rebids 2NT. Partner is showing you a 12-14 hand with a club stopper. You should therefore pass. **Answer:** (a) Pass.

PART IV

ADVANCED BIDDING

12

FOURTH SUIT FORCING

In Chapter 3 on the opener's rebid, we noted that when an auction starts with bids in three suits (for example, 1♡ - 1♠; 2♣), neither player has limited his hand. On many deals the responder will be able to make a limited bid at his second turn. For example, he might pass or bid 2♡ or 2♠ to sign off. With a better hand he could bid 3♣, 3♡ or 3♠ to invite a game. All those bids are limited and define the strength of responder's hand within a narrow range of points.

When instead the responder wants to play at the game level (at least) and needs further time to investigate the best denomination (which trump suit or notrump), he can use a special gadget. He makes an artificial bid in the fourth suit, 2♢ here. This convention is known as **fourth suit forcing**. Note that the 2♢ bid says absolutely nothing about what diamonds the responder holds. If he held good diamonds he might have bid 3NT instead.

Fourth suit forcing to look for the best game

Let's see a typical auction involving a fourth-suit bid:

WEST	EAST	WEST	EAST
♠ A Q 8 7 2	♠ 10 3	1♠	2♢
♡ Q J 7 5 4	♡ A K 6	2♡	3♣
♢ 5	♢ K Q J 6 2	3♡	4♡
♣ A 8	♣ 9 7 2		

Look at East's predicament at his second turn. With 13 points opposite an opening bid he wants to play in game, yes, but which game? He cannot bid 3NT with only ♣972 in the unbid suit and he cannot raise hearts with only three-card support. He bids the fourth suit (here 3♣) to pass this message: 'I am good enough for a game contract (at least) but I need further information.' Here West bids his heart suit again, showing five, and East is then able to raise to 4♡.

To get familiar with the idea, let's see another fourth-suit auction.

WEST	EAST	WEST	EAST
♠ 8	♠ A J 7 6 2	1◇	1♠
♡ A 10 3	♡ Q 6	2♣	2♡
◇ A Q 10 7 2	◇ K 6 5	2NT	3NT
♣ Q 9 8 2	♣ K 10 3		

Once again East has no sensible natural bid to make at his second turn. He cannot rebid 3◇ because this would not be forcing. Remember this: *when you are strong enough for a game contract, you must either bid a game or make a forcing bid.* One of the saddest remarks you hear at the bridge table is: 'Sorry, I hoped you would bid again.'

To ensure that the auction will continue to game, East bids 2♡ (fourth suit forcing). West bids 2NT to show his stopper in hearts and East is happy to raise to 3NT.

You can see from these examples that a bid in the fourth suit does not promise any length or high-card strength in the suit that you have bid. Indeed, if you did have a good holding in that suit, you would probably have bid notrump instead.

Fourth suit forcing with a fit for partner

Let's see another important application of this very useful gadget. It arises when you have a fit for one of your partner's suits but you are too strong to make a limited bid in that suit:

WEST	EAST	WEST	EAST
♠ A Q 10 7 5	♠ 7 3	1♠	2♣
♡ A J	♡ 10 4 3	2◇	2♡
◇ Q 10 7 2	◇ A J 9 6	2NT	3NT
♣ 9 5	♣ A K 7 5		

East is too strong for a limit raise to 3◇, which might result in a missed game. He shows his strength by bidding the fourth suit and awaits further information from his partner. When West shows a heart stopper by bidding 2NT, there is no reason for East to show his diamond support (even though 3◇ via the fourth suit would be forcing). He is happy to raise to 3NT.

Let's see another example of this use of fourth suit forcing:

WEST	EAST	WEST	EAST
♠ 6	♠ A K J 2	1♡	1♠
♡ A Q 10 7 2	♡ K J 8	2♣	2♢
♢ Q J 5	♢ 10 9 4 3	2NT	3♡
♣ K 8 6 5	♣ A 9	4♡	

What can East bid at his second turn? He wants to show his heart support but 3♡ would be non-forcing, while jumping to 4♡ might result in a missed slam.

The solution is to bid a fourth suit forcing 2♢. East can then bid a forcing 3♡ on the next round. This shows a good hand because with fewer high cards he would have bid 3♡ or 4♡ on the second round. On this occasion West's hand is nothing special and he signs off in game. With a stronger hand, where a slam looked promising, he might have asked for aces or made a control-showing cuebid (see Chapter 14).

Fourth suit forcing when responder has a good suit

A similar situation may arise when the responder holds a strong hand with a long suit of his own. Suppose he has responded 1♠ initially. If he rebids 2♠ or 3♠, this will be a non-forcing limited bid. To ensure that game is reached, he can make a fourth suit forcing bid before bidding his long suit again.

WEST	EAST	WEST	EAST
♠ 10 4	♠ A K J 9 7 5	1♢	1♠
♡ 7	♡ Q 9 2	2♣	2♡
♢ A Q J 7 2	♢ K 3	3♣	3♠
♣ K Q 7 6 2	♣ J 8	4♠	

Again East seems to have a bidding problem at his second turn. A rebid of 3♠ would not be forcing. Remember that it is a principal rule of good bidding that you must not make a non-forcing bid below game level when your hand is good enough for game.

East bids a fourth suit forcing 2♡ and rebids his spades on the next round. West raises to game in spades and the best contract is found.

Responding to fourth suit forcing

Most of the time it will be fairly obvious what to bid next after partner's fourth suit forcing bid. Let's look briefly at some situations where the best action may not be clear.

Suppose you have a stopper in the fourth suit. Given the bidding space, should you bid 2NT or 3NT? The auction is forcing to game, so you will normally bid only 2NT. This will allow partner the opportunity to tell you at the three-level what sort of hand he has. He may want to show support for one of your suits or perhaps rebid a strong suit of his own. You should go to 3NT only when you have a double stopper in the unbid suit and are fairly sure that this will be the right contract.

WEST	EAST	WEST	EAST
♠ A 10 9 6	♠ Q 3	1◇	1♡
♡ 5	♡ A K J 9 6 2	1♠	2♣
◇ K 10 8 6 3	◇ Q 9 2	3NT	
♣ A Q 9	♣ 7 3		

With a solid ♣AQ9 in the fourth suit, you are happy to leap all the way to 3NT. You are not interested in hearing about possible diamond support or a promising heart suit.

The best continuation may not be clear on this West hand:

WEST	EAST	WEST	EAST
♠ K 4	♠ A Q J 7 5	1♡	1♠
♡ A Q 10 7 6	♡ 5 4	2◇	3♣
◇ K 9 6 4	◇ A J 2	3♠	4♠
♣ 10 3	♣ J 7 2		

Partner already knows that you hold five hearts. You cannot bid notrump or rebid the diamonds. The best you can do is to bid 3♠, showing something in that suit. Partner will have no reason to expect a 3-5-4-1 hand since you might well have raised to 2♠ on that shape.

Fourth Suit Forcing — Problems A

1.   ♠ A Q 9 6 3 ♡ A 7 5 ◇ K 8 2 ♣ 9 5

The bidding starts 1◇ - 1♠; 2♣. What will you say next, as responder?

   (a) 2♡   (b) 3◇   (c) 3NT

2.   ♠ 9 ♡ A Q 5 ◇ 9 7 3 ♣ A Q J 8 5 2

The bidding starts 1♠ - 2♣; 2◇. What will you say next, as responder?

   (a) 2♡   (b) 3♣   (c) 3NT

3.   ♠ K Q 9 6 2 ♡ A 1 0 8 7 ◇ 7 5 ♣ Q 5

The bidding starts 1◇ - 1♠; 2♣. What will you rebid as responder?

   (a) 2♡   (b) 2NT   (c) 4♡

4.   ♠ 2 ♡ A J 9 8 4 ◇ K Q 6 ♣ A Q 1 0 5

The bidding starts 1♡ - 1♠; 2♣ - 2◇. What will you say next as the opener?

   (a) 2NT   (b) 3♡   (c) 3NT

5.   ♠ Q 7 2 ♡ A K 1 0 6 5 ◇ 4 ♣ A Q 8 7

The bidding starts 1♡ - 1♠; 2♣ - 2◇. What will you say next as opener?

   (a) 2♠   (b) 2♡   (c) 3♠

(*The answers are overleaf.*)

Fourth suit forcing — Solutions A

1.   ♠ A Q 9 6 3   ♡ A 7 5   ◊ K 8 2   ♣ 9 5

The bidding starts 1◊ - 1♠; 2♣. You want to be in game but have no idea which game will be best. It's a perfect hand for fourth suit forcing and you bid 2♡. According to partner's rebid and the subsequent auction, you may end up in 3NT, 4♠ or 5◊. Occasionally partner will be strong enough for a slam. Note that 3◊ would not be forcing and 3NT would simply be a guess at the best spot. **Answer:** (a) 2♡.

2.   ♠ 9   ♡ A Q 5   ◊ 9 7 3   ♣ A Q J 8 5 2

The bidding starts 1♠ - 2♣; 2◊. A rebid of 3♣ would not be forcing. Since you have a double stopper in hearts, you are happy to bid 3NT now. Suppose you had the ◊A instead of the ◊9. With such a strong hand there would then be a good chance of a slam. You would bid a fourth suit forcing 2♡, looking for more information from your partner. **Answer:** (c) 3NT.

3.   ♠ K Q 9 6 2   ♡ A 10 8 7   ◊ 7 5   ♣ Q 5

The bidding starts 1◊ - 1♠; 2♣. You should not bid 2♡ now. Firstly, remember that it would not show anything in hearts. Secondly, a fourth suit forcing bid is game-forcing and you are not quite strong enough for that. You should rebid 2NT, a limit bid that invites a game and shows a stopper in the unbid suit. **Answer:** (b) 2NT.

4.   ♠ 2   ♡ A J 9 8 4   ◊ K Q 6   ♣ A Q 10 5

The bidding starts 1♡ - 1♠; 2♣ - 2◊. Partner has made a fourth suit forcing bid. You are happy to bid notrump on your ◊KQ6 but should you bid 2NT or 3NT? No contest! You should bid 2NT. The bidding is forcing to game, remember, so you do not have to bid 3NT to ensure game is reached. Also, partner may have various reasons to bid 2◊. Perhaps he wants to show strong support for your hearts or clubs, or to rebid a good spade suit. Leave him the space to do this. **Answer:** (a) 2NT.

5.   ♠ Q 7 2   ♡ A K 10 6 5   ◊ 4   ♣ A Q 8 7

The bidding starts 1♡ - 1♠; 2♣ - 2◊. Although 2♠ would be forcing, this would not make it clear to your partner what useful support you have for his spades. He will nearly always hold at least five spades on this auction and a spade slam is very likely. You should jump to 3♠ to give partner the good news. **Answer:** (c) 3♠.

Fourth Suit Forcing — Problems B

6.   ♠7 ♡AQ874 ◇A 10 9 8 5 ♣A 5

The bidding starts 1♡ - 1♠; 2◇ - 3♣; 3◇ - 3♡. What will you say next, as responder?

(a) 4♣   (b) 4♡   (c) 4♠   (d) 4NT

7.   ♠Q 6 5 ♡KQ 9 8 2 ◇9 7 ♣A 6 3

The bidding starts 1◇ - 1♡; 1♠. What will you say next, as responder?

(a) 2♣   (b) 2♡   (c) 2NT   (d) 3♡

8.   ♠KJ 9 5 3 ♡AJ 8 7 3 ◇AJ ♣4

The bidding starts 1♠ - 2♣; 2♡ - 3◇. What will you say next?

(a) 3♡   (b) 3NT   (c) 4♡

9.   ♠10 2 ♡KQ 7 6 ◇AQ 9 7 2 ♣Q 4

The bidding starts 1♠ - 2◇; 2♡. What will you say next as responder?

(a) 3♣   (b) 3♡   (c) 4♡

10.   ♠7 ♡AKJ 10 5 3 ◇K 3 ♣AQ 9 2

The bidding starts 1♡ - 1♠; 2♣ - 2◇. What will you say next as opener?

(a) 2♡   (b) 2NT   (c) 3♡

(The answers are overleaf.)

Fourth Suit Forcing — Solutions B

6.   ♠7 ♡A Q 8 7 4 ◇A 10 9 8 5 ♣A 5

The bidding starts 1♡ - 1♠; 2♡ - 3♣; 3◇ - 3♡. Partner has heart support but he did not show it on the previous round. Ask yourself: why was that? It's because he was too strong to bid 3♡ or 4♡. He wanted to suggest a heart slam. Your hand is great for slam purposes! You hold three aces and the queen of trumps. The best bid now is actually 4♣ — a cuebid that shows the ♣A and interest in a slam. 'How on earth am I meant to know that?' your reaction may be. You're right. We will discuss cuebids in the final chapter of the book. If you decided to bid 4NT instead, to ask for aces and head towards 6♡, that is equally good. **Answer:** (a) 4♣ or (d) 4NT.

7.   ♠Q 6 5 ♡K Q 9 8 2 ◇9 7 ♣A 6 3

Partner opens 1◇, you respond 1♡ and he bids 1♠. This type of hand is awkward to bid. You have the values for a game try, and you would like to show partner your fifth heart. Should you make a fourth suit forcing bid of 2♣? No! That would be game-forcing. Your two value bids are 2NT (showing your club stopper) and 3♡ — but the latter would imply a decent six-card suit, which you do not have. **Answer:** (c) 2NT.

8.   ♠K J 9 5 3 ♡A J 8 7 3 ◇A J ♣4

The bidding starts 1♠ - 2♣; 2♡ - 3◇. Partner's fourth suit forcing bid asks you to describe your hand further. You have a fifth card in hearts, also a diamond stopper, and must choose between 3♡ and 3NT. It is better to rebid the hearts, ensuring that you do not miss a 5-3 fit in that suit. **Answer:** (a) 3♡.

9.   ♠10 2 ♡K Q 7 6 ◇A Q 9 7 2 ♣Q 4

The bidding starts 1♠ - 2◇; 2 ♡. There is no need to bid a fourth suit forcing 3♣ on this hand. A straightforward raise to 4♡ will describe your hand admirably. **Answer:** (c) 4♡.

10.   ♠7 ♡A K J 10 5 3 ◇K 3 ♣A Q 9 2

The bidding starts 1♡ - 1♠; 2♣ - 2◇. Although 2♡ would be forcing, you describe your hand much better with a leap to 3♡, telling partner that you have an excellent six-card heart suit. This may pave the way to a good slam in hearts. **Answer:** (c) 3♡.

13

SLAM BIDDING

To make a small slam, your combined holdings need both power and controls — the power to make twelve tricks and the controls (aces, kings, singletons and voids) to prevent the defenders from cashing two tricks first. Look at these two hands:

WEST	EAST
♠ A Q 10 9 6 3	♠ K J 5 2
♡ K Q 5	♡ A 3
◇ J 4	◇ 10 7 2
♣ A 3	♣ K Q 9 7

Suppose you bid to 6♠. You have plenty of power: six spade tricks, three hearts and three clubs. Unfortunately, the slam will fail on a diamond lead because you can't prevent the defenders from scoring the first two tricks in that suit.

Now let's see two hands where you have all the suits well controlled; indeed, the defenders cannot cash a single trick at the start. However, you cannot make a slam because you do not have the necessary power.

WEST	EAST
♠ K 6 3	♠ A 8 2
♡ A K Q 5	♡ J 10 7 6
◇ A 6 4	◇ K 9 3
♣ A 9 6	♣ K J 7

Imagine for a moment that you're in 6♡. You have all the aces and kings in the deck, yes, but you have only ten tricks. A successful club finesse might give you an eleventh trick, but the slam would still be a very poor one.

Accurate slam bidding is not easy. First you have to assess whether you have the power to produce twelve tricks. When either player sees that there is playing strength to spare, beyond that needed for game, he can consider a slam.

Bidding a slam after a jump shift

When your partner opens the bidding and you hold around 19 points or more, a slam may well be possible — particularly if you can find a trump fit.

WEST	EAST	WEST	EAST
♠ J 8 4	♠ A K Q 7 6 3	1♦	2♠
♡ 6	♡ K Q 5	3♠	4NT
♦ A Q 8 6 4	♦ K J 2	5♡	6♠
♣ A Q 9 6	♣ 7		

East starts with a jump shift of 2♠, showing a good spade suit and a hand worth 19 points or more. West is happy to support spades and East is then confident that the two hands will produce twelve tricks. He needs to check that West has two aces, to make sure that the defenders cannot cash the first two tricks. He does this by using the **Blackwood** convention, bidding 4NT to ask partner how many aces he holds. No doubt you are already familiar with this table:

BLACKWOOD RESPONSES

5♣	0 or 4 aces
5♦	1 ace
5♡	2 aces
5♠	3 aces

On the deal above, West shows two aces and East jumps to 6♠. The slam is a good one. The defenders can make the ♡A but declarer will score the remaining tricks.

If the 4NT bidder is contemplating a grand slam, he can continue with 5NT to ask for kings. The responses are the same as above but at the six-level.

Bidding a slam with extra values

Take the East cards here and see how you view the situation:

WEST	EAST	WEST	EAST
♠ Q J 6 2	♠ A K 10 9 5	1♡	1♠
♡ K Q J 7 6	♡ A 4	4♠	4NT
♦ A K	♦ 10 8 2	5♦	6♠
♣ Q 5	♣ K 9 3		

What should your reaction be when partner rebids 4♠? Do you pass and think 'I should make this easily!'? Let's hope not. Your partner wanted you to play at the game level even if you held a minimum 6-point response with only four spades. Not only do you hold five magnificent trumps, you also have a second ace and a total of 14 points. You have so much to spare that a slam will surely be a good contract. You bid 4NT, finding partner with one ace, and jump to a small slam in spades. The ♣A is the only trick that the defenders can make.

It is not usually a good idea to use Blackwood when you have two or more top losers in a suit. However, West has shown a strong hand and will surely hold a diamond control.

How do you judge whether you have enough extra values to play in a slam rather than a game? It's not just a question of counting points. Good trumps are always welcome, particularly extra length in the trump suit. Aces and kings are important too, with humble queens and jacks less likely to prove vital. The longer you play the game, the better you will be able to judge whether your hand justifies a slam try.

Bidding a slam after a 2♣ opening

When partner opens 2♣ and rebids in a suit, he is saying that he wants to play at the game level (at least) even if you hold nothing of value. When you hold a useful card or two, you are entitled to head slamwards.

WEST	EAST	WEST	EAST
♠ A K Q 6 2	♠ 5 4	2♣	2◇
♡ A K J 7 6	♡ Q 10 8 3	2♠	2NT
◇ A 3	◇ K 8 5 2	3♡	4♡
♣ J	♣ K 9 4	4NT	5♣
		6♡	

East's 2NT bid has already shown some (limited) values, so there is no need for East to bid more than 4♡. West settles for 6♡ when he finds out that an ace is missing. The final contract is an excellent one, as you see.

WEST	EAST	WEST	EAST
♠ K Q	♠ 5 4	2♣	2◇
♡ A K 7	♡ 10 8 6 3	3♣	3◇
◇ K 3	◇ A Q 10 5 2	3NT	6NT
♣ A K Q 9 6 5	♣ J 7		

West shows a very powerful hand with long clubs. East has every right to raise the bar to 6NT. There are eleven tricks on top and a twelfth trick can easily be established from the spade suit.

WEST	EAST	WEST	EAST
♠ A Q 10 5	♠ K J 7 6	2♣	2◇
♡ K J 2	♡ Q 10 9 3	2NT	3♣
◇ K Q J 5	◇ A 4	3♠	6♠
♣ A Q	♣ J 5 3		

When East discovers a 4-4 spade fit, he calculates that the combined hands will be enough for 6♠. So it proves. Twelve tricks will be easy once declarer has drawn trumps and forced out the ♡A.

Bidding a slam in notrump

When two balanced hands face each other, you need around 33 HCP to bid 6NT and 37 to bid 7NT. Auctions such as 1NT - 6NT are commonplace, with the responder merely adding his points to those shown by the opener. When responder needs an upper-range opening to justify bidding 6NT, he can invite a slam by responding 4NT (this is not Blackwood when it is a raise of a natural notrump bid):

WEST	EAST	WEST	EAST
♠ K 9 5 2	♠ A 8 6	1NT	4NT
♡ A K 7 4	♡ Q 2	6NT	
◊ A 2	◊ K J 7 5		
♣ Q J 6	♣ A K 9 4		

East holds 17 HCP and would like his partner to play in 6NT if he has 16 or 17 HCP opposite. He passes this message by responding 4NT. West has a maximum 17 HCP and accepts the try, raising 4NT to 6NT. There are eleven tricks on top and several good chances of setting up a twelfth trick. (At an early stage declarer will duck a round of spades to test for a 3-3 break in that suit.)

Let's see what would happen if West did not hold quite such a good hand.

WEST	EAST	WEST	EAST
♠ K 10 5 2	♠ A 8 7	1NT	4NT
♡ A J 7 4	♡ Q 2	pass	
◊ A 2	◊ K J 7 5		
♣ Q J 6	♣ A K 9 4		

West has a minimum 1NT opening of 15 HCP and rejects the invitation. There are nine tricks on top and an easy tenth trick can be established in hearts. 6NT would require a considerable amount of luck and would not be a good contract.

From the deals we have seen, you will realize that slam bidding is not a precise art. When a slam is likely to be a good prospect, take the plunge and bid it. Sometimes making the slam will be easy. Other times it may need a finesse or a favorable lead. Occasionally the slam may prove to be a bad one on the cards that partner happens to hold. Don't let the occasional failure prevent you from bidding slams in future.

Slam Bidding — Problems A

1.

EAST	WEST	EAST
♠ A Q 8 6 2	1♡	1♠
♡ Q 6	3♡	?
◇ A 10 8 7		
♣ K J		

Do you think a slam is likely after your partner's 3♡ rebid? What will you bid next?
    (a) 3NT   (b) 4♡   (c) 4NT   (d) 6♡

2.

EAST	WEST	EAST
♠ Q 9 7 5	1♡	1♠
♡ 9 6	3♠	?
◇ A K J 5		
♣ Q J 7		

Do you think a slam is likely after your partner's 3♠ rebid? What will you bid next?
    (a) 3NT   (b) 4♠   (c) 4NT   (d) 6♠

3.

EAST	WEST	EAST
♠ 4		1◇
♡ 7 5	2♡	3♣
◇ A K J 6 5	3♡	?
♣ A K 9 7 3		

Do you think a slam is likely after your partner's 3♡ rebid? What will you bid next?
    (a) 4♣   (b) 4♡   (c) 4NT   (d) 6♡

4.

EAST	WEST	EAST
♠ A 6	2NT	?
♡ K Q 7		
◇ J 9 8 6 2		
♣ Q 10 7		

Your partner's 2NT shows 20-21 points. What response will you make?
    (a) Pass   (b) 4NT   (c) 6NT

(The answers are overleaf.)

Slam Bidding — Solutions A

1.   ♠ A Q 8 6 2   ♡ Q 6   ◇ A 10 8 7   ♣ K J

The bidding starts 1♡ - 1♠; 3♡. Partner has suggested at least 16 points with his jump rebid. You have 16 HCP, which puts you in the slam zone. What's more, you hold some good cards. The ♡Q will be very valuable and you have two precious aces. You intend to bid 6♡ but you might as well bid 4NT (Blackwood) on the way, just in case you are missing two aces. **Answer:** (c) 4NT.

2.   ♠ Q 9 7 5   ♡ 9 6   ◇ A K J 5   ♣ Q J 7

The bidding starts 1♡ - 1♠; 3♣. You have some points to spare for a raise to 4♠ but the prospects for a slam are not particularly good. Look at your weak trumps! Only four of them and they are headed by just one honor. You have no heart honor to help set up partner's suit and you hold only one ace. It is best to be conservative on such a hand, raising to 4♠. If you were slightly stronger you might cuebid 4◇. As we will see in the next chapter, this would invite a slam and show the ◇A. **Answer:** (b) 4♠.

3.   ♠ 4   ♡ 7 5   ◇ A K J 6 5   ♣ A K 9 7 3

The bidding starts 1◇ - 2♡; 3♣ - 3♡. Partner has shown a very powerful hand (19 or more points) with a splendid heart suit. The prospects for slam are splendid, since you are bringing two A-K combinations to the party and partner may well be able to score a spade ruff or two as well. If partner has the ♠A and the ♡AK, 7♡ should be a very good contract, and may well be laydown. Blackwood will tell you whether or not this is the case. **Answer:** (c) 4NT.

4.   ♠ A 6   ♡ K Q 7   ◇ J 9 8 6 2   ♣ Q 10 7

Partner opens 2NT, showing 20-21 points. It is not possible to bid the hand precisely because much will depend on whether your partner has a useful diamond holding opposite your five-card suit. The best you can do is to respond 4NT, asking partner to bid 6NT when he holds 21 points and to pass with 20. **Answer:** (b) 4NT.

Slam Bidding — Problems B

5.

EAST	WEST	EAST
♠ A J 8 6 2	3♡	?
♡ K 6 4		
◇ A K Q 10		
♣ 9		

Do you think a slam is likely after your partner's 3♡ preempt? What will you bid next?

      (a) 3♠   (b) 4♡   (c) 4NT   (d) 6♡

6.

EAST	WEST	EAST
♠ A Q J 6 3	1◇	1♠
♡ 9 6	2♡	?
◇ Q 7		
♣ A K J 7		

Do you think a slam is likely after your partner's bidding? What will you bid next?

      (a) 3♣   (b) 3NT   (c) 4NT   (d) 6NT

7.

EAST	WEST	EAST
♠ A 4		2♣
♡ A K Q 10 7 5 2	2◇	2♡
◇ Q 6	3♣	3♡
♣ A K	4♡	?

West's 3♣ is a second negative. Do you think a slam is likely after this bidding? What will you say next?

      (a) Pass   (b) 4NT   (c) 5♡   (d) 6♡

8.

EAST	WEST	EAST
♠ J 5 3	2♣	2◇
♡ 5 2	2♠	?
◇ 9 8 7 4		
♣ Q 6 4 3		

What action will you take now, as responder?

      (a) Pass   (b) 3♠   (c) 4♠

(*The answers are overleaf.*)

Slam Bidding — Solutions B

5.   ♠ A J 8 6 2   ♡ K 6 4   ◇ A K Q 10   ♣ 9

Your partner opens 3♡. If he holds seven hearts headed by the ace, you will have a good chance of scoring seven heart tricks and four top winners in the side suits. A twelfth trick may come from a club ruff or the ◇10, even if partner has no other useful card. You should respond 4NT to see if partner holds an ace. Even if this happens to be the ♣A, you will have a good chance of making twelve tricks.
Answer: (c) 4NT.

6.   ♠ A Q J 6 3   ♡ 9 6   ◇ Q 7   ♣ A K J 7

The bidding starts 1◇ - 1♠; 2♡. Partner has reversed and will hold around 17 points or more. You hold 17 HCP. Although there is no great trump fit, you can expect there to be good play for slam on a combined total of at least 34 points. Since you cannot be missing two aces after partner's strong bidding, there is little point in using Blackwood, although it would not be wrong to do so. You could simply bid 6NT, which will likely be a good contract. However, spades may play better, and opposite the right hand from partner, you may even be able to make seven. Start with 3♣, fourth suit forcing, and see whether partner can support spades.
Answer: (a) 3♣.

7.   ♠ A 4   ♡ A K Q 10 7 5 2   ◇ Q 6   ♣ A K

Your partner's 3♣ is a second negative. He cannot have either the ◇A or ◇K and make this bid. If you advance to the five-level, there is every chance that you will lose a spade and two diamonds, going one down. You should pass.
Answer: (a) Pass.

8.   ♠ J 5 3   ♡ 5 2   ◇ 9 8 7 4   ♣ Q 6 4 3

The bidding starts 2♣ - 2◇; 2♠. Partner's rebid is forcing to game, so there is no question of passing on your hand. You should go directly to 4♠, which indicates a weak hand with no ace or king. Suppose you held ◇A984 instead of ◇9874. You would then make the more encouraging raise to 3♠. Knowing that you held at least one good card in your hand, partner might then try for a slam.
Answer: (c) 4♠.

Slam Bidding — Problems C

9.

WEST	WEST	NORTH	EAST	SOUTH
♠ A J 8 4		3◇	3♠	5◇
♡ Q 9 6 4	?			
◇ —				
♣ A 10 9 7 6				

What will you bid next?

(a) Dbl   (b) 5♠   (c) 6♠

10.

WEST	WEST	EAST
♠ A J		1◇
♡ J 7 6 3	1♡	4♡
◇ J 5 4		
♣ K Q 8 5		

Do you think a slam is likely after your partner's bidding? What will you bid next?

(a) Pass (b) 4♠ (c) 4NT (d) 5♡ (e) 6♡

11.

WEST	WEST	EAST
♠ A K	2♣	3♣
♡ A K J 7 6 4	3♡	3NT
◇ K Q	?	
♣ A J 7		

Do you think a slam is likely after this bidding? What will you say next?

(a) Pass (b) 4♣ (c) 4♡ (d) 6♣

12.

WEST	WEST	EAST
♠ A K 7 6 2		1◇
♡ K 3	1♠	3◇
◇ Q 7 4	?	
♣ A 10 5		

Do you think a slam is likely after this bidding? What will you say next?

(a) 4◇ (b) 4NT (c) 5◇ (d) 6◇

(The answers are overleaf.)

Slam Bidding — Solutions C

9.   ♠ A J 8 4   ♡ Q 9 6 4   ◇ —   ♣ A 10 9 7 6

The bidding start (3◇) - 3♠ - (5◇). You have a fabulous hand in support of spades. Your void in diamonds will prevent the opponents from taking any diamond tricks. It is losing bridge to think 'We might have two losing hearts.' Your thoughts should run along these lines: 'We are surely likely to make a slam here. It would be much too timid to bid just 5♠ and risk missing the slam bonus.' **Answer:** (c) 6♠.

10.   ♠ A J   ♡ J 7 6 3   ◇ J 5 4   ♣ K Q 8 5

The bidding starts 1◇ - 1♡; 4♡. Are you tempted to look for a slam? Partner wanted to play in 4♡ when you might hold only 6 points and you actually have 12 HCP. That's true, but there are two factors that should warn you against bidding on. Your trumps (♡J763) are alarmingly weak. There is a big risk that you may have two trump losers, even if the other suits are watertight. Also, your diamond holding will not help much in avoiding a loser in that suit. You have only 2 points in partner's long suits. Although there might be a good slam available, the odds are against it and you should pass. **Answer:** (a) Pass.

11.   ♠ A K   ♡ A K J 7 6 4   ◇ K Q   ♣ A J 7

The bidding starts 2♣ - 3♣; 3♡ - 3NT. Your partner has given a positive response in clubs, showing a good suit. He surely holds something like ♣KQxxxx. In that case 6♣ will be an easy make. Even if no diamond ruff in your hand is available, partner will be able to set up your heart suit. You should bid 4♣, agreeing clubs as trumps. We will see in the next chapter how you can actually check to see whether partner has the ◇A and the ♣KQ, in which case a grand slam will be possible. **Answer:** (b) 4♣.

12.   ♠ A K 7 6 2   ♡ K 3   ◇ Q 7 4   ♣ A 10 5

The bidding starts 1◇ - 1♠; 3◇. Partner's rebid shows 16-18 points. You hold 16 HCP and have a good fit for his six-card diamond suit. The scent of an excellent slam is in the air! You should head for 6◇. We will look at some advanced slam-bidding techniques in the next chapter. For the moment, it scarcely matters which route you take towards the slam. **Answer:** (a) 4◇, (b) 4NT or (d) 6◇.

14

RKCB AND CUEBIDDING CONTROLS

Experienced players use two very valuable aids to slam bidding: Roman Keycard Blackwood (RKCB) and control-showing cuebids. In this final chapter of the book we will give a brief description of these methods.

Roman Keycard Blackwood (RKCB)

In addition to the four aces, there are two other cards that can be critical when you are considering a slam contract: the king and queen of trumps. Roman Keycard Blackwood (RKCB) is a modern variant of Blackwood that allows you to find out about these trump cards as well as the four aces. When using this convention, there are five **keycards** — the four aces and the trump king. The response to 4NT will indicate how many keycards responder holds:

5♣	1 or 4 keycards
5◇	0 or 3 keycards
5♡	2 keycards, without the trump queen
5♠	2 keycards, with the trump queen

A 5♣ response shows more keycards than 5◇ (unlike in traditional Blackwood). To remember the meanings of 5♣ and 5◇ think of 1430 — the score at duplicate for a vulnerable major-suit slam.

Over a 5♣ or 5◇ response, the 4NT bidder may bid the cheapest non-trump suit to ask for the trump queen. The responder signs off in the trump suit without that card, otherwise shows his cheapest side-suit king or, with no side kings, bids 5NT. Alternatively, the 4NT bidder may continue with 5NT to ask partner how many kings he holds outside the trump suit (6♣=0, 6◇=1, 6♡=2, 6♠=3).

This is all a bit complicated, yes, and this is why we have left it until the very last chapter. However, it does allow you to bid slams with far greater accuracy. Even if you don't intend to play RKCB at the moment, you may find it interesting to take a look at it, noting the exciting methods available to you in due course.

Right, let's see some examples of Roman Keycard Blackwood in action:

WEST	EAST	WEST	EAST
♠ 10 7	♠ A K Q 8 6	1♡	1♠
♡ A K 9 7 4 2	♡ Q 8 5	2♡	4NT
♢ J 8	♢ K Q 10 2	5♢	6♡
♣ A 4 3	♣ 7		

West is likely to hold six hearts on this auction. East bids RKCB and the response shows 0 or 3 keycards. It is impossible for West to have 0, since he opened the bidding. Whether West holds two aces and the ♡K or three aces, there will be good play for the slam. East duly leaps to 6♡, which will easily be made.

Next let's see how RKCB can stop you bidding a bad slam.

WEST	EAST	WEST	EAST
♠ A 9 7 4	♠ Q 8 6 3 2	1♢	1♠
♡ 3	♡ A K J	3♠	4NT
♢ A Q J 8 7 2	♢ K 6 4	5♢	5♠
♣ Q J	♣ K 10		

With a powerful hand facing a jump rebid, East is entitled to assume that the playing strength is present for a slam. Before bidding 6♠, he needs to check that two keycards are not missing. When he bids 4NT he hears that partner holds two keycards (without the trump queen). Since East holds only one keycard, he knows that two of the five are missing. Either two aces are missing, or one ace and the ♠K. In neither of these cases does he wish to be in a slam contract. He therefore signs off in 5♠. Note that we want to have four keycards to be in a small slam, and all the keycards to consider investigating a grand slam.

Finally, we will see two examples of asking partner whether he holds the queen of trumps:

WEST	EAST	WEST	EAST
♠ 7 2	♠ A K 6 4 3	2♡	4NT
♡ A J 8 6 5 2	♡ K 10	5♣	5♢
♢ Q J 8	♢ 5	5♡	
♣ 10 5	♣ A K Q J 2		

West opens with a weak 2♡. East can see that 6♡ will be a good contract if West's trumps are headed by the ace and queen. He bids 4NT, hearing of one keycard, which is probably the ♡A. He continues with 5♢, the cheapest non-trump bid, asking 'Do you hold the ♡Q?' Since West does not hold that vital card, he signs off in 5♡, which becomes the final contract. If West did hold the ♡Q, he would either cuebid a side-suit king (5♠, 6♣ or 6♢) or bid 5NT (with no side-suit king).

WEST	EAST	WEST	EAST
♠ A Q J 10 7 2	♠ K 6 5	1♠	2♣
♡ A 8 3	♡ K 10	3♠	4NT
◇ A J	◇ K 10 4 2	5◇	5♡
♣ 9 6	♣ A K Q 7	5NT	7NT

West bids RKCB with spades agreed as trumps. The 5◇ response shows three keycards. 5♡, the next available non-trump bid, asks for the ♠Q. The response of 5NT says: 'I have the ♠Q and no side-suit king.' East can count six spade tricks, two hearts, two diamonds and three clubs. He bids 7NT with confidence.

Cuebidding a control

Although you may initially find it a tricky concept to master, cuebidding a control to show slam interest and an ace in a side suit is an indispensable part of good slam bidding. Suppose the bidding starts like this:

West	East
1♡	1♠
3♠	4◇

West's jump to 3♠ sets spades as the agreed trump suit. What can 4◇ possibly mean? There would be no point in it showing a diamond suit, since you have already found a good trump suit.

When a trump suit has been agreed, a bid in a new suit (usually at the four-level) is a cuebid. It shows the ace of the suit you have bid and interest in a slam.

In the auction above, East's 4◇ passes two messages, 'I am interested in a spade slam' and 'I hold the ◇A.' In fact, it also passes a third message 'I do not hold the ♣A', since he would show his cheapest ace (in other words, one that he could show with the lowest bid). Let's see how the whole auction might go after this start:

WEST	EAST	WEST	EAST
♠ A J 7 6	♠ K Q 8 4 3	1♡	1♠
♡ A K 9 7 4	♡ 8 5	3♠	4◇
◇ 8 2	◇ A K 10 6	4NT	5♠
♣ A 4	♣ 7 6	6♠	

East suggests a slam and West is happy to accept. As we explained in the last chapter, using Blackwood or RKCB with two small cards in a suit is not a good idea. That is why East could not launch into RKCB directly over 3♠. However, once partner has assured him that he holds the ◇A, West can use RKCB, as he knows diamonds are under control

Sometimes both players make cuebids:

WEST	EAST	WEST	EAST
♠ K J 7 6	♠ A 3	1NT	3♡
♡ K 7 5	♡ A Q 10 6 4 2	4♣	4♢
♢ K Q 8 2	♢ A 9 6	4NT	5♢
♣ A 4	♣ 10 8	6♡	

East's 3♡ shows at least six hearts and suggests a slam. It would not make any sense for West's 4♣ to be natural — it is a cuebid showing a control. It says that West's hand is suitable for a heart slam and he holds the ♣A. East is not quite certain that he wants to bid a slam but he makes the encouraging move of showing the ♢A. West then uses RKCB on his way to 6♡ — an excellent contract.

In the above auction, it was the cuebid (4♣) that agreed hearts as trumps. There was no ambiguity about the meaning of the bid because a natural 4♣ would make no sense on a balanced hand.

Do you remember Problem 11 in the quiz for the previous chapter? It featured the West hand here:

WEST	EAST	WEST	EAST
♠ A K	♠ 7 6 3	2♣	3♣
♡ A K J 7 6 4	♡ 2	3♡	3NT
♢ K Q	♢ A 9 6	4♣	4♢
♣ A J 7	♣ K Q 10 8 5 4	4NT	5♠
		7♣	

We recommended 4♣ as the best bid for West over 3NT. Opposite this particular East hand, you can see how the bidding would develop. With clubs agreed as trumps, East cuebids the ♢A. West uses RKCB and hears that East has two keycards (the ♢A and ♣K) plus the ♣Q. It is then easy to bid the grand slam.

RKCB and cuebidding controls — Problems A

1.
WEST	WEST	EAST
♠ A K 9 8 6 5	1♠	3♠
♡ A 5	?	
◇ Q 7 6		
♣ A J		

Do you think a slam is likely after your partner's 3♠? What will you bid next?

(a) 4♣　　　(b) 4♠　　　(c) 4NT　　　(d) 6♠

2.
WEST	WEST	EAST
♠ A 10	1♡	4NT
♡ K 9 7 6 3	?	
◇ A 6 4 2		
♣ J 7		

What will you bid next after partner's 4NT bid?

(a) 5♣　　　(b) 5◇　　　(c) 5♡　　　(d) 6♡

3.
WEST	WEST	EAST
♠ A Q 10 9 3	1♠	2♣
♡ K 4	2◇	4♠
◇ A K 6 4	?	
♣ Q 2		

Do you think a slam is likely after your partner's bidding? What will you say next?

(a) Pass　　　(b) 4NT　　　(c) 5◇　　　(d) 6♠

4.
WEST	WEST	EAST
♠ A 6		2♠
♡ 7	?	
◇ A K Q J 2		
♣ A 10 8 5 4		

What is your bidding plan on this hand? What response will you make?

(a) 4♣　　　(b) 4♠　　　(c) 4NT　　　(d) 6♠

(*The answers are overleaf.*)

RKCB and cuebidding controls — Solutions A

1.   ♠ A K 9 8 6 5   ♡ A 5   ◇ Q 7 6   ♣ A J

The bidding starts 1♠ - 3♠. A slam is possible but you are not certain you want to go so high. Blackwood will not help much, and in any case is not advisable with no diamond control in your hand. What you want to do is to *suggest* a slam and see how partner reacts. You can do this by bidding 4♣. This shows the ♣A and suggests a slam. If partner bids 4◇ next, showing the ◇A, you can bid 4♡ to tell him about the ♡A. Perhaps he will then be willing to bid 4NT. If instead he decides to sign off in 4♠, you will pass. This is how slam auctions should proceed, with both partners involved in the decision making. **Answer:** (a) 4♣.

2.   ♠ A 10   ♡ K 9 7 6 3   ◇ A 6 4 2   ♣ J 7

The bidding starts 1♡ - 4NT. Partner's response is RKCB with hearts agreed as trumps. You have three keycards, so your response is 5◇ (showing 0 or 3 keycards). Remember the 1430 acronym. **Answer:** (b) 5◇.

3.   ♠ A Q 10 9 3   ♡ K 4   ◇ A K 6 4   ♣ Q 2

The bidding starts 1♠ - 2♣; 2◇ - 4♠. Partner has shown a sound raise to the spade game and you have plenty of values to spare, including a possibly useful queen in his main suit (clubs). You should bid 4NT to check that partner holds at least two of the three missing keycards. If he does, you will bid 6♠. **Answer:** (b) 4NT.

4.   ♠ A 6   ♡ 7   ◇ A K Q J 2   ♣ A 10 8 5 4

Your partner opens 2♠. If he holds six spades headed by the K-Q, a small slam should be a good contract. You start by bidding RKCB. If partner shows two keycards (♠K and ♡A) without the ♠Q, you will bid only 6♠. If he shows two keycards with the ♠Q, you can bid 7♠ (or 7NT). If partner responds 5♣, showing only one keycard, you will need to bid 5◇ to ask for the queen of trumps. If partner denies this card, you will pass his 5♠, and otherwise bid 6♠. **Answer:** (c) 4NT.

RKCB and cuebidding controls — Problems B

5.

EAST	WEST	EAST
♠ 6	2♣	2♡
♡ K Q 8 7 5 2	3♡	?
◇ A 7 6		
♣ 9 7 4		

Do you think a slam is likely after your partner's 3♡ raise? What will you bid next?

(a) 4◇　　　(b) 4♡　　　(c) 4NT　　(d) 6♡

6.

EAST	WEST	EAST
♠ A Q 6 3		1◇
♡ J 6	1♠	3♣
◇ A K 7 6	4NT	5◇
♣ A 7 3	5♡	?

What has the auction meant so far? What will you bid next?

(a) 5♠　　　(b) 5NT　　　(c) 6◇　　　(d) 6♠

7.

EAST	WEST	EAST
♠ K 4		3♡
♡ K Q J 8 7 6 2	4NT	5♣
◇ 10 4	5NT	?
♣ 6 3		

What will you bid now?

(a) 6♣　　　(b) 6◇　　　(c) 6♡

8.

EAST	WEST	EAST
♠ A Q 10 7 4 2		1♠
♡ A 10 3	2NT	3♠
◇ 9 8	4♣	?
♣ K Q		

What does partner's bidding mean? What will you bid now?

(a) 4◇　　　(b) 4♡　　　(c) 4♠　　　(d) 4NT

(The answers are overleaf.)

RKCB and cuebidding controls — Solutions B

5.   ♠6 ♡KQ8752 ◇A76 ♣974

You hold a useful hand opposite a 2♣ opener. What is more, you have found a good trump fit. You are surely heading for at least a small slam in hearts. At this stage you should show partner the ◇A by bidding 4◇. **Answer:** (a) 4◇.

6.   ♠AQ63 ♡J6 ◇AK76 ♣A73

The bidding starts 1◇ - 1♠; 3♠ - 4NT; 5◇ - 5♡. What does that all mean? Your 3♠ showed a strong hand in support of spades and 4NT was RKCB. Your 5◇ response showed 0 or 3 keycards (presumably three in view of your strong bidding). Partner's 5♡ continuation, the cheapest non-trump bid, is asking for the ♠Q. The possible responses are 5♠ (sign-off, no ♠Q), 5NT (♠Q but no side-suit king), 6♣/6◇/6♡ (♠Q and your cheapest side-suit king). **Answer:** (c) 6◇.

7.   ♠K4 ♡KQJ8762 ◇104 ♣63

The bidding starts 3♡ - 4NT; 5♣ - 5NT. Partner's RKCB 4NT asked for keycards and your 5♣ response showed one (the ♡K). You could not hold four keycards when you opened with a preempt. Partner's 5NT continuation is asking how many side-suit kings you hold. You would bid 6♣ with none and must now bid 6◇ to show one side-suit king. **Answer:** (b) 6◇.

8.   ♠AQ10742 ♡A103 ◇98 ♣KQ

The bidding starts 1♠ - 2NT; 3♠ - 4♣. Partner's 2NT was Jacoby 2NT, showing at least a sound game-raise in spades. Your 3♠ rebid showed extra values but no side-suit singleton. Spades are agreed as trumps and 4♣ is a control-showing cuebid. Partner is showing the ♣A and interest in bidding a slam. You have six good trumps and excellent cards for a slam. You indicate your enthusiasm by bidding 4♡, which shows the ♡A and denies the ◇A. (When cuebidding you always show the cheapest ace on the bidding ladder first.) **Answer:** (b) 4♡.

RKCB and cuebidding controls — Problems C

9.
EAST	WEST	EAST
♠ A J 8 7	2♣	2◇
♡ 10 5	2♠	3♠
◇ 9 8 5 2	4◇	?
♣ A 7 4		

What will you bid next?

    (a) 4♠   (b) 4NT   (c) 5♣   (d) 6♠

10.
EAST	WEST	NORTH	EAST	SOUTH
♠ K 9 7 6				3♡
♡ 6	4♠	pass	?	
◇ Q J 8 5				
♣ A 10 7 3				

What action will you take?

    (a) Pass   (b) 4NT   (c) 5♣   (d) 6♠

11.
EAST	WEST	EAST
♠ K 9 4		1NT
♡ A Q 8 6	3♠	?
◇ 10 4		
♣ A K 8 4		

Partner's 3♠ shows six-plus spades and suggests a slam. What will you bid now?

    (a) 3NT   (b) 4♣   (c) 4♠   (d) 4NT

12.
EAST	WEST	EAST
♠ A J 6 5 4 2	1◇	1♠
♡ K 10 3	4♠	?
◇ 8		
♣ K Q 7		

What does partner's bidding mean? What will you bid now?

    (a) Pass   (b) 4NT   (c) 5♠   (d) 6♠

(The answers are overleaf.)

RKCB and cuebidding controls — Solutions C

9.   ♠ A J 8 7   ♡ 10 5   ◇ 9 8 5 2   ♣ A 7 4

The bidding starts: 2♣ - 2◇; 2♠ - 3♠; 4◇. Partner's 4◇ shows the ◇A and suggests a slam. With two aces facing a 2♣ opening, and a good trump fit already found, you must ensure that a slam is reached. To bid 4♠ now would be a bad mistake. (Such a bid would not show the ♠A, of course; a cuebid is made only in a side suit. 4♠ would be a sign-off). You should bid 5♣ to show partner the ♣A. Since you have little idea what his hand looks like, you should not take control of the auction by bidding 4NT. **Answer:** (c) 5♣.

10.   ♠ K 9 7 6   ♡ 6   ◇ Q J 8 5   ♣ A 10 7 3

Your LHO opens 3♡ and partner overcalls 4♠. This is a strong bid, since your opponent has shown a weak hand. Add in your values (good trump support, the singleton heart, the ♣A and the lower honors in diamonds) and the chances of a slam are excellent. You are entitled to bid 6♠ provided two keycards are not missing. **Answer:** (b) 4NT.

11.   ♠ K 9 4   ♡ A Q 8 6   ◇ 10 4   ♣ A K 8 4

The bidding starts 1NT - 3♠. Partner has long spades and is suggesting a slam. Your hand could hardly be more splendid in support of spades. If you had a doubleton spade and relatively few controls, you might bid 3NT to tell partner you did not fancy a slam. With spade support in a minimum hand with few controls, you would raise to 4♠. Here you must bid more ambitiously. The best bid is 4♣. This cannot possibly be a natural bid when you have opened 1NT and partner has shown six-plus spades. It is a cuebid, showing the ♣A and telling partner that you like the idea of a slam. **Answer:** (b) 4♣.

12.   ♠ A J 6 5 4 2   ♡ K 10 3   ◇ 8   ♣ K Q 7

Partner has gone all the way to 4♠ when you might hold only 6 points — he promises 19-20 points. You have plenty of values to spare, not least a six-card trump suit. You are worth a RKCB 4NT bid. If partner holds at least three keycards you will bid 6♠ (your singleton opposite partner's long suit does not make 7♠ attractive). Note that the trump fit is expected to be 6-4, so you will not need to check for the ♠Q. If that card is missing it will probably drop under the ace and king. Or if South shows out when you play dummy's ♠K, you can catch North's ♠Qxx with a finesse. **Answer:** (b) 4NT.

GLOSSARY OF BRIDGE BIDDING TERMS

A

Agreement An understanding between partners as to the meaning of a particular bid. 'We have an agreement that opposite an overcall a new suit will be forcing.'

Artificial bid A bid with a special meaning. For example, an opening 2♣ does not show clubs but announces a very powerful hand.

B

Balanced hand A hand that has 4-3-3-3, 4-4-3-2 or 5-3-3-2 shape.

Balancing A bid made in the passout seat. 'South's 1♠ was followed by two passes and East then balanced with 2◊.'

Balancing seat When the bidding will end if you pass, you are said to be in the balancing (or passout) seat. The responsibility of contesting the auction is yours.

Blackwood A 4NT bid that asks partner how many aces he holds.

Bonus Contracts at a high level attract a bonus in the scoring. For example, 4♠ is a game contract and gives you a game bonus. A contract of 6NT attracts a slam bonus.

C

Call In addition to a bid, such as 1NT or 2♠, the term 'call' includes pass, double and redouble.

Cheapest bid The next available bid. The cheapest bid over 5◊ is 5♡.

Competitive Bidding When both sides enter the auction

Control When you are contemplating a slam, it is important that you should have a control in each suit to prevent the defenders from cashing the ace and king. A control can be an ace, a king, a singleton or a void.

Convention A bid that has an artificial meaning unrelated to the suit named. For example, in the Stayman convention a response of 2♣ to 1NT asks for four-card majors.

Cuebid	(1) A bid in a suit bid by an opponent. Such a bid always indicates strength. (2) Once a trump suit has been agreed, a bid in a new suit (usually at the four- or five-level) shows slam interest and the ace of that suit.

D

Double	A call that may have many different meanings, according to the context. For example, it may be a **penalty double**, or a **takeout double** (see glossary entries).
Double raise	A raise of partner's suit by two levels (1♠ - 3♠). Such a raise shows a stronger hand than a single raise.
Dummy points	See **Support points**.

E

Extra values	Values, such as HCP or shape, beyond those that your bidding has already described.

F

Five-card majors	Most systems world-wide treat an opening bid of 1♡ or 1♠ as showing at least five cards. 'We play five-card majors.'
Forcing bid	A bid that forces partner to bid again (unless an opponent intervenes with a bid).
Fourth suit forcing	A strength-showing artificial bid by the responder in the only remaining unbid suit. In the sequence 1◇ - 1♠ - 2♣ - 2♡, for example, the responder's 2♡ is fourth suit forcing. It is game-forcing and asks the opener to continue to describe his hand.

G

Game-forcing	A bid or bidding sequence that ensures your side will advance to at least a game contract.
Game try	A bid that suggests bidding a game and asks partner to make the decision. For example, after a start of 1♠ - 2♠ you might bid 3◇. This suggests a spade game, at the same time telling partner that you hold diamond length.
Good fit	The situation in a trump contract where the side-suit holdings combine well. For example, Axx or 9xx opposite a singleton is a good fit; KQx or QJx opposite a singleton is not.

H

HCP
High card points, the standard count where aces/kings/queens/jacks are worth 4/3/2/1 points respectively.

High reverse
A non-jump bid in a third suit at the three-level. In the sequence 1♠ - 2◇ - 3♣, for example, 3♣ is a high reverse and is forcing to game.

Holding
The cards held in a suit. 'My club holding was ace-queen doubleton.'

I

Intermediate cards
Spotcards such as tens and nines, which increase the playing strength of a hand.

Invite game
When you are uncertain whether to bid a game, you can choose a bid to invite game. After a start of 1◇ - 1♠ - 2◇, responder's 2NT shows 11 or 12 points and invites a game.

J

Jacoby 2NT
Facing a 1♡ or 1♠ opening, you can use Jacoby 2NT to show that you hold four or more cards in partner's suit and at least 13 points.

Jump preference
In an auction such as 1◇ - 1♠ - 2♣ - 3◇, responder has shown jump preference for diamonds. He likes diamonds better than clubs and he holds invitational values.

Jump raise
A raise of partner's suit one level higher than the minimum possible raise, for example 1♠ - 3♠.

Jump rebid
A rebid of a player's original suit one level higher than the minimum possible rebid. For example, 1♡ - 1♠ - 3♡ shows a stronger hand than a rebid of 2♡.

Jump response
Opposite a takeout double, a single jump (for example a response of 2♠ to a double of 1◇) shows around 9-11 points.

Jump shift
A change-of-suit bid one level higher than is necessary (for example, 1♡ - 2♠, or 1◇ - 1♡; 2♠.)). A jump shift promises 19+ points and is game-forcing.

K

Keycards
When a trump suit has been agreed and a slam investigation is underway, there are five keycards: the four aces and the king of trumps.

L

LHO Abbreviation of 'left-hand opponent', the player sitting on your left.

Limited bid A bid that defines the strength of your hand within narrow limits. If partner opens 1♠, for example, the responses of 1NT and 2♠ are limited bids.

Limit raise A raise of 1♡ to 3♡ (or 1♠ to 3♠) is known as a limit raise. It shows about 10-12 points and invites partner to continue to the major-suit game.

M

Minimum hand A hand containing only the bare requirements for a bid. For example, a 1NT opening on 15 HCP.

Misfit The situation where a partnership's hands do not contain a trump fit of eight cards or more.

N

Natural bid A bid that shows length in the suit shown. Compare with **artificial bid**.

Negative double A takeout double of an overcall. For example in the sequence 1◊ - 1♠ - Dbl, the responder's double is negative. In this case it strongly suggests four cards in hearts, the unbid major.

New suit A suit that has not previously been bid.

O

Opener's rebid The opener's second bid.

Opening bid The first bid made in an auction.

Overbid A bid that exaggerates the values actually held. 'West's 4♠ was a bad overbid.'

Overcall A bid made after an opponent has opened. 'South opened 1♡ and West overcalled 2◊.'

Overtrick A trick scored beyond the number needed to make the contract.

P

Partscore A contract below the game level.

Passout seat	When the preceding two players have passed, you have the chance to close the auction by passing.
Passed hand	A player who has previously declined to open the bidding and whose strength is therefore known to be limited.
Penalty double	A double made when you think that the opponents' contract will fail and want to increase the stakes.
Playing strength	A hand contains good playing strength if it has the ability to create a large number of tricks. It might, for example, have a suit such as KQJ1076.
Preemptive bid	A bid made on a weak hand with a long suit, or a good trump fit for partner. The objective is to deprive the opponents of bidding space.
Preemptive raise	A raise made on a weak hand with the objective of depriving the opponents of bidding space. For example, when partner opens 3♠ and you raise to 4♠ this might be a sound raise; it might equally well be a preemptive raise.
Preference	When partner has shown two suits and you have a minimum hand, you will often tell him which of his suits you prefer. In the auction 1♡ - 1♠ - 2♣ - 2♡, responder is 'giving preference to hearts'.

Q

Queen-ask	After a 5♣ or 5♢ response to RKCB 4NT, you can continue with the next non-trump bid to ask whether partner holds the queen of trumps.

R

Raise	When you have a fit for a suit that partner has bid, you may raise his suit. For example if he opens 1♡, you may raise to 2♡.
Rebid	One meaning is the second bid made by a player. 'South opened 1♠ and rebid 2♡'. A second meaning is to bid a suit twice. 'South rebid his diamonds'.
Redouble	When an opponent has doubled, you are permitted to redouble. In the sequence 1♠ - dbl - redbl, for example, the responder tells his partner that he holds at least 10 points and it may be possible to make a penalty double of the opponents' eventual contract.

Rescue bid	If partner has been doubled for penalties, it will sometimes be appropriate for you to rescue him by bidding a long suit of your own.
Responder	The partner of the opening bidder. Also, the player who must find a bid opposite a takeout double or a Blackwood enquiry.
Responder's rebid	The second bid made by the opener's partner.
Response	A bid made in reply to a bid from your partner. 'West opened 1◊ and East responded 1♠.'
Reverse bid	A rebid by the opening bidder that carries the auction past the safety level of two of his suit (for example, 2♡ in 1◊ - 1♠ - 2♡). Such a rebid shows extra values.
RHO	Abbreviation of 'right-hand opponent', the player sitting on your right.
Roman Keycard Blackwood	An artificial 4NT bid that asks partner how many keycards he holds. Generally shortened to RKCB.

S

Sacrifice	A contract bid in the expectation of going down. The aim is to lose fewer points than you would if the opponents' contract was made. 'When they bid 4♡, we sacrificed in 4♠.'
Second negative	Suppose the bidding starts 2♣ - 2◊ - 2♡ (or 2♠). The responder can then bid 3♣, a second negative, to show that he has a very weak hand. Any other rebid will show some values.
Shape	The shape of a hand is the number of cards in each of the suits. 'Since I had 4-4-3-2 shape, I opened 1NT.'
Sign off	Attempt to close the auction. 'Partner made a game try but I signed off in 3♠.'
Simple overcall	An overcall made at the minimum level, for example 2♣ over 1♡.
Single raise	A raise of partner's suit by one level, for example 1♡ - 2♡. Such a raise shows around 6-9 points.
Stayman	Opposite a 1NT bid a Stayman 2♣ asks partner if he holds a four-card major. The objective is to locate a 4-4 major-suit fit.
Stopper	A holding that may prevent the opponents from running winners in a suit, for example ♠K8 or ◊Q105.
Stopper bid	When a minor suit has been agreed, a bid in a new suit at the three-level shows that you hold a stopper there for a possible notrump contract.

Strong 1NT	Around the world, the most popular range for a 1NT opening is 15-17 HCP.
Support	To agree partner's suit as trumps. When the bidding starts 1♡ - 2♡, for example, the responder has supported the opener's hearts.
Support points	Once a trump fit has been found, the value of your hand has two components — HCP and support points. You are entitled to value your hand more highly if it contains a shortage (doubleton, singleton or void) that may provide a ruffing opportunity.

T

Takeout double	A double that requests partner to choose a trump suit (or notrump), also to give an indication of his strength. Nowadays, most doubles below the game level are for takeout.
Trump fit	Although it is not always possible, you should look for a combined trump length of at least 8 trumps.

U

Unbalanced hand	A hand containing a singleton or void.

W

Weak 1NT	An alternative 12-14 range for a 1NT opening, which has a minority following in North America.
Weak jump overcall	An overcall that skips one level. An overcall bid of 2♠ over an opening bid of 1♢, for example, suggests a hand similar to a weak 2♠ opener.
Weak two-bid	An opening bid of 2♢, 2♡ or 2♠ that shows a six-card suit and 6-10 points.
Weak three-bid	An opening bid of 3♣, 3♢, 3♡ or 3♠ that shows a seven-card suit and insufficient strength to open with a one-bid. The intention is to remove bidding space from the opponents.

Master Point Press on the Internet

www.masterpointpress.com

Our main site, with information about our books and software, reviews and more.

www.teachbridge.com

Our site for bridge teachers and students — free downloadable support material for our books, helpful articles and more.

www.bridgeblogging.com

Read and comment on regular articles from MPP authors and other bridge notables.

www.ebooksbridge.com

Purchase downloadable electronic versions of MPP books and software.